HIKING
in
TOPANGA
STATE PARK

*This illustration is of Janet and Bob Solum
hiking in Santa Ynez Canyon*

Hiking
in
Topanga
State Park

by

MILT McAULEY

Illustrated by Janet Solum

CANYON PUBLISHING CO.

Canyon Publishing Company
8561 Eatough Avenue
Canoga Park, CA 91304

Acknowledgements

This third edition of Hiking in Topanga State Park, first written in 1981, leans heavily upon the first edition. Although the book has been changed, those people who contributed to the original version are important to me and are appreciated. They are: Park Rangers Greg Nelson, Debbie Brodrick, and Don Richardson; Edie Cooper; Bill Crane; Jim Kenney; Dan Larson; Sue Othmer; Janet Solum; Ron Webster; Dale Wilson; and Maxine McAuley.

Table of Contents

Eagle Rock

Introduction

Welcome to this mountain park—bound on the north by the Santa Monica Mountain crest, on the south by Pacific Palisades and Brentwood, on the west by the deep Topanga Canyon, and on the east by the remote Rustic Canyon. With a staunch bulwark of rock and chaparral successfully holding back the population expansion, Topanga State Park offers adventure, excitement, and isolation from the bustle of city life. Conceived of ocean deposits and born of compressive land forces, these mountains have seen fire and flood, and have grown through volcanic action and earthquake.

Come along with me on a trip into the Park. We'll see spectacular waterfalls, travel challenging trails, and savor the beauty of hundreds of acres of California lilacs. We will make our way across ridges, down into canyons and meet head-to-head the stillwild land unchanged since the days Indians walked their trails. We will explore water-sculpted sandstone cliffs in the Santa Ynez Canyon and climb to the foot of magnificent rocky bastions which stand like sentinels guarding the land—all this within the city limits of Los Angeles. The first spring flowers will delight us as they unfold to their fullest glory. A grassy slope under the oaks will invite us to kick back and relax, and on a clear day we can even see Catalina Island. You will discover what it is like to live with the wilderness in our backyard.

So come on an adventure, walk the trails, absorb the history, let the mountains work their magic, and experience the friendship that awaits you.

A steep, gravelly trail leads up and into the "cathedral."
Isolated inside and protected from the wind, twenty-five
hikers can have lunch together.

TOPANGA STATE PARK

TOPOGRAPHY

Topanga State Park, 10,000-plus acres of wildland in the central Santa Monica Mountains, is located almost totally within the city limits of Los Angeles, California. No other city in the world harbors an equal area of natural parkland. Astride the east-west trending Santa Monica Mountains, Topanga State Park offers a recreational wilderness to hundreds of thousands of people within walking distance, and to millions more within a few miles.

Access to the Park is provided through entry points from streets leading north of the western end of Sunset Blvd., Topanga Canyon Blvd., and Mulholland Drive. Within the Park a network of fireroads, firebreaks and trails allows further access for the hiker or equestrian.

The Park terrain is determined by three canyons that run north to south. Topanga Canyon on the west, Santa Ynez Canyon in the center, and Rustic Canyon on the east dictate a north-south trail structure in the southern part of the Park. An east-west ridge at the head of Santa Ynez Canyon and another at the head of Temescal Canyon make cross travel possible. The northern boundary of the Park lies close to the east-west ridge of the Santa Monicas and is traversed by Mulholland Drive. Trails on most of the ridges and some of the canyons afford access to all but a few remote pockets of the Park.

Steep slopes and sharp ridges dominate the view. Except for some oak woodlands on the gentler slopes and riparian woodlands in the streambeds, the Park is covered with chaparral. Travel by other than established trail or fireroad is virtually impossible.

The skyline features ridges and peaks, the highest of which is Temescal Peak at 2126'. High in the center of the Park, Cathedral Rock is a prominent and distinctive formation. An amphitheater in its center can comfortably seclude a hiking group for a lunch stop. A few miles away, Eagle Rock is a favorite viewing spot. A cave on top provides protection from sun and weather, and the view of the canyon below is spectacular. The ridge between Topanga Canyon and Santa Ynez Canyon can be walked its entire length, affording a continuous change of scenery with views of cliffs, canyons, and finally the ocean.

Down in the canyons, the scope of view is limited, but each turn of the trail brings new delights. The waterfalls, rock shelters, variety of plant life, and caves in the sandstone cliffs all may be inspected at close range. The wooden tank at Eagle Spring, the remnants of the limestone quarry in Quarry Fork, and the two stone chimneys at the Old Cabin Site add an historical flavor to the Park. Upper Temescal Canyon is in pristine shape. No trails or other access routes enter it and travel is difficult. It is an outstanding example of wildland as it has been for centuries. The variety of topographic features adds a rich dimension to a visit in the Park.

The chimney of the old cabin site in Santa Ynez Canyon

PLANT LIFE

The vegetation of the Park is an important natural resource. It is vital to the animal community because it forms the basis for the food chain. Ground cover and a deep root system stabilize the soil and reduce erosion by wind and rain. Living plants as well as the leaves and other remains that fall to the ground retard water runoff, restraining floods and mud slides. An equally important value of plants is the sight and smell offered to all who enter the mountains. Every spring brings a riot of flowers to the streambeds and hillsides. Even the burned-over areas—or I should say particularly the burned-over areas—respond to the winter rains with a display of native flowers brought to life from seed that has lain dormant for many years. The chaparral covered areas of the Park produce an annual eruption of thousands of acres of California lilac trees in bloom that overwhelm the senses. Starting in January, the blooming climaxes late in March with white and blue, sweetly pungent blossoms. A spring day in the chaparral reacquaints me with the beauty of this forest.

The plant life in Topanga State Park can be divided into 6 distinct communities, each having recognizable characteristics. They are: (1) Chaparral, (2) Oak woodlands, (3) Riparian woodlands, (4) Grasslands, (5) Coastal sage scrub, and (6) Cliffside.

M.M. '81

White alder

Alnus rhombifolia

CHAPARRAL

Chaparral is a nearly impenetrable, dense cover of stubborn shrubs which grow on poor, dry, rocky soils. The name "chaparral" comes from the Spanish word chaparro, which describes a thicket of dwarf evergreen oaks; here chaparral applies to a plant community of a wide variety of hard, thick, broad-leaved plants. Some almost pure stands of type (or specie) of plants can be found but usually the chaparral is a diverse community of several hundred varieties, about 25 of which are dominant. Typical chaparral plants found in the Park are ceanothus (or California lilac), chamise, chaparral currant, chaparral yucca, fuchsia-flowered gooseberry, holly-leaf cherry, holly-leaf redberry, laurel sumac, mountain mahogany, poison oak, scrub oak, sugar bush, and toyon.

Chaparral covers most of the steep slopes and ridges in a dense tangle of closely spaced bushes and shrubs. It grows on rocky or sandy soil that drains well, as the roots cannot tolerate moisture for extended periods of time. Wet, mild winters to promote active spring growth, and long, hot dry summers for dormancy are essential. Ecologically the many plant species of the chaparral are similar, but most are unrelated toxonomically. A dual root system is characteristic with surface roots using moisture that penetrates the top few inches of soil and the tap roots reaching deep into the soil to support the plant during a long dry season.

3/81
M.M.

Chamise

Adenostoma
fasciculatum

The leaf form is a distinctive feature of the chaparral, being small, thick, stiff, and evergreen. Deciduous plants lose their leaves and are unable to use the moisture from the occasional summer thunder shower or early autumn rainstorm. They must develop a new crop of leaves before the new moisture supply can be used. Being evergreen makes chaparral plants opportunists; they begin photosynthesizing immediately upon absorbing moisture. This is important in the spring because having leaves gives them a head start. Repeated fires have been a prominent factor in the evolution of the chaparral. Many of the plants have adapted to fire by crown-sprouting after being burned to the ground New sprouts develop from the root system, and the plants regenerate quickly. Some plants grow from seeds that will germinate only after a fire has split the outer seed coat. Viability of some seeds is claimed to last a hundred years or more.

Scrub oak

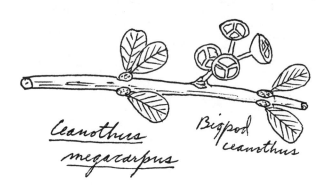

Ceanothus megacarpus

Bigpod ceanothus

OAK WOODLANDS

The oak woodland plant community is an oak-dominated area, usually on sloping hillsides, but sometimes at the edge of flat grasslands. Coast live oaks form this plant community in Topanga State Park. Trippet Ranch is centered in a large oak woodland that merges with chaparral on the steeper slopes and abuts the open grassland north of the Ranch. Ground cover is often grass and a wide variety of small plants such as giant wild rye, poison oak, pitcher sage, purple nightshade, phacelia, sage and some of the chaparral plants. The California walnut tree is often an important member of the woodland and in some places is the dominant tree. The oak woodland plant community supports a wide variety of animal life.

Coast live oak
Quercus agrifolia

M.M. '81

RIPARIAN WOODLANDS

This plant community is confined to stream bottoms where there is a year round source of water. The woodland is made up of a variety of ferns, mosses, vines and shrubs under a canopy of sycamore, coast live oak, willow, California bay, and occasionally broadleaf maple. The well-developed multiple vegetation layers include the tree canopy, the shrub layer, and herb layer. A wide variety of both plant and animal life lives in the riparian woodlands. The several forks of the Santa Ynez Canyon are beautiful examples of this plant community, as is Temescal Canyon. Blackberry, poison oak and mugwort form much of the ground cover. Look for six foot high Humboldt lilies along the stream banks in late spring. The

stream and the dense plant cover provide a home for newts, salamanders, frogs and all those unidentified water beetles seen in the stream. Deer, raccoons, coyotes and the other large animals visit the stream—tracks can be found on mud banks, scat on trails, and once in a while the animal can be sighted. The riparian woodland is a rare and precious place; Topanga State Park is indeed blessed.

California laurel
or
Bay

GRASSLANDS

Less than 2% of the Santa Monica Mountains is classified as grassland; the largest areas being at the western end in Point Mugu State Park where some stands of native bunch grass are thriving. The grass in Topanga State Park, other than giant wild rye, is mostly introduced annual species that came into California with the arrival of the Spaniards. I've heard that sailors dumped straw out of their mattresses and renewed the filling, thus seeding the local area. I've also heard that seeds in horse manure from horses fresh from off the ship could have been the cause, but find that hard to believe. More likely, grass seeds were mixed in with the grain seeds brought in to plant the mission fields. With grazing pressure from domesticated animals the annuals out-competed and largely replaced the native perennial grassland. Recently, annual grass seeds have been sown by aircraft after fires in some areas. The State Park lands have not been subjected to this practice, and the natural plant life in Topanga State Park has protected the burned surfaces without interference from the reseeding of introduced species.

The Dead Horse Trail crosses the southern edge of this grassland

COASTAL SAGE SCRUB

This plant community is not restricted to the immediate coast, but is often found inland. The coastal sage community is mixed association of California sagebrush, California buckwheat, encelia, lemonade berry, sugar bush, laurel sumac, purple sage, black sage, perennial grasses, chaparral yucca, and flowers. Quite often coastal sage and chaparral merge together with pockets of one being found in the other plant community. Coastal sage often occupies disturbed sites in the chaparral.

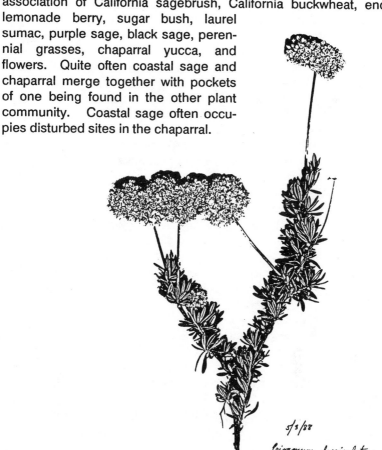

5/3/88

Eriogonum fasciculatum

CLIFFSIDE

Cliffs and the rock debris at their base provide a harsh environment for plant life. Some species thrive on this adversity and are found on the many rock outcroppings throughout the Park. Some characteristic plants are: dudleya, golden yarrow, shrubby bedstraw, Tejon milk-aster, spike moss, bricklebush, and fuchsia. Silver lotus is found on Eagle Rock and Cathedral Rock.

GEOLOGY

The Santa Monica Mountains are geologically young. 10 million years ago compressive forces folded and faulted the land, thrusting it out of the sea in an east-west series of wrinkles that we now call the Santa Monica Mountains.

The development of the Santa Monica Mountains began approximately 180 million years ago when clay particles were carried out to sea and deposited on the floor of the ocean to eventually become Santa Monica slate—the bedrock of much of the mountains. Granitic intrusions forced their way into the earth's crust after the slate had been deposited, thereby making slate and granite the oldest rocks to be found in the Santa Monicas. The land was covered by a shallow sea for most of its history, and a succession of mudstone, siltstone, and sandstone was deposited until now about 35 bedrock layers can be identified.

About 40 million years ago, the land rose out of the sea and became a flood plain on which a formation of sandstone and conglomerate was laid down. This hard, cliff-forming rock combination is the Sespe formation which is named for an extension of the same layer found near Sespe Creek north of the Santa Clara River. Following the non-marine period of building, the land was once more covered by the sea, and thousands of feet of sedimentary rock were formed.

About 15 million years ago, during the sedimentary process, volcanic activity, which lasted for 2 million years, caused igneous rocks to intrude through the sandstone. Near the end of the volcanic activity a deep trough, possibly 5,000 feet deep, developed in part of the area, and fine particles settled to the bottom of the ocean to form the Modelo formation which consists of shaly diatomaceous mudstone, and siltstone, and layers of sandstone. The Modelo formation is the last bedrock unit to be formed in the Santa Monica Mountain area, except for scarce outcroppings of gray shale and sandstone named the Pico formation.

As these layers of rock were forced together creating a mountain range, 10 million years of rain, flood and earthquake gouged out canyons, created peaks and ridges, and altered the mountains to the form they have today.

Many of the geological formations of the Santa Monica Mountains can be found in Topanga State Park. Faults can be located; marine fossils are evident; volcanic intrusions are prominent, and a wide variety of sedimentary formations can be see on the hikes.

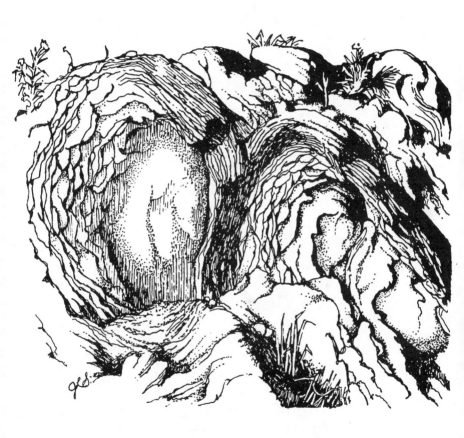

An example of volcanic intrusion seen near Eagle Rock Road. The concentric exfoliation of the diabase rock suggests the name "onion rock."

Red-tailed Hawk

Bobcat

Coyote

Cottontail

Mule Deer

Mountain Lion

Gray Fox

Calif Ground Squirrel

22

ANIMAL LIFE

Upon walking the backcountry of the Park you not only enter the plantlife arena but also the home of the animals. Usually very little activity is apparent; a few birds glide down the slope; lizards sun themselves; a stir 30 feet away in a patch of sage, or a fly buzzes around your ear, but nothing to get excited over. It is true that you may pass by unheralded, but not unnoticed. The soaring redtailed hawk sees every movement long before he himself is seen; a deer may silently circle through the brush and return to the same spot after you have passed; no one knows how often a bobcat has watched from a ridge then silently backed down the other side when a hiker neared; if you hear the yip-yip of a coyote he may be down in the canyon while you are up on a ridge, or vice versa. He is seldom seen, though always there. There is one exception to this silent reception—the scrub jay who scolds loudly if you rest in his favorite grove.

The wildlife in the Park is cautious and makes every effort to remain hidden, and with just cause. People, dogs, and domestic goats have invaded the natural environment of the native animals, upsetting the traditional balance to some degree. Dogs leave their scent and disturb the territorial claims of coyotes. They also chase everything in sight including deer, the preferred food of mountain lions.

For a period during the early 80's the Park was the site of an experimental program using goats to crop the vegetation on fire-breaks. Some displacement of grass and weed-eating animals may have taken place. Prior to the goats, bulldozers scraped the land leaving opportunities for soil erosion and the complete destruction of natural vegetation. Now, with the exception of some vegetation abatement, nature is allowed to run its course. With favorable results, I might add.

The urbanization of the mountains started almost two centuries ago and continues to take a toll in animal life at an increasing rate. Bears no longer range this territory (and it could be truthfully said that not many people miss them); mountain lions have been driven to the most remote areas; the last condor in the mountains was seen from Topanga in 1937 and it most likely had flown in from one of the roosting areas in the Topatopa Mountains, and even deer are sometimes hard to find. Many animals do live in the Park; a list is found in the appendix. You will find lizards sunning during the heat of the day, quail feeding in the fringe area of chaparral, red-tailed hawks soaring overhead, and other birds looking for seeds and insects on the ground.

Frog or toad—how do you tell them apart? Easy—frogs have smooth skin, toads don't. Also, the front toes are without webs, and the hind toes are webbed. Two types of frogs and one type of toad are commonly found in the Santa Monica Mountains and the Park: The Pacific Treefrog *(Hyla regilla)*, The California Treefrog *(Hyla cadaverina)*, and the Western Toad *(Bufo boreas)*. Several other frogs, including the Bullfrog *(Rana catesbeiana)*, a species introduced from the midwest, are found occasionally but are not numerically significant.

The Pacific Treefrog is small — 3/4 inch, sometimes more — but never considered large until the "kreck-eck" of the call is heard coming from a pond or streambed. The voice may sound large, but look for a small inoccuous brown, green, or any color in-between, narrow-headed frog with a black eye stripe. The Pacific Treefrog can be found any time of the year in the Park, but never far from water. He, as well as the California Treefrog, is more evident during the mating season (January to July). Toward twilight the first Pacific Treefrog hesitatingly quavers out a "kreck-eck"; then bolstered with courage, all the males cut loose. A few days later the first cloud of frogs' eggs appears on the pond—then tadpoles—and all this because one frog went "kreck-eck."

Pacific Tree Frog

24

The California Treefrog is about the same size as the Pacific Treefrog and is gray, sometimes with dark blotches, but no eye stripe. In the Park, California Treefrogs match the Topanga sandstone in color and are hard to find. Usually hiding behind a rock along a stream, this frog sets up a flat sounding "quack," tempting you to imitate it. Your reward for a good imitation will be the sight of a small frog or two hopping toward you.

The horned lizard suns itself in the dust or on a rock, changing its shade of gray to match the terrain. This peaceful animal tries to look ferocious but can't quite scare anything larger than its own three to four inch length.

Rattlesnakes are important residents of the Park. Like all reptiles, they are unable to internally control their own body temperature so they seek a place that will heat them when cold and cool them when hot. They hibernate underground during winter and come out in spring when the temperature reaches 75° - 80° for several days in a row. This usually happens during the last half of February. Heavy winter rains will sometimes drive them out.

A Southern Pacific Rattlesnake in Rustic Canyon

The high water in Big Sycamore Creek during the winter of 1979-1980 left some rattlesnakes on the beach. There is no speculation on how many swam out to sea. During spring rattlesnakes are usually out during the day, keeping warm and looking for a meal. During the heat of summer, they stay in the shade and come out in the evening for as long as the temperature is high.

Birds are plentiful in the Park and the careful observer can see them everywhere except in mature chaparral, where they are scarce and usually hidden. The time to hear them best is between four and six in the morning; but one need not hear to enjoy, so even the ten o'clock scholar can enjoy the birds. Guided bird-watching tours are a regular feature of the Park.

Coyotes take the urban dream in stride. They keep out of sight when people are around but then hang around the edge of civilization to steal a chicken or cat from the careless. Just after sundown I have heard coyotes yipping down in Garapito Canyon when I was on the ridge near Eagle Rock. I expect that if I had been down in the canyon the coyotes would have been on the ridge. Although seldom seen, their presence is evident.

Coyotes show no modesty when they deposit their "scat" in the middle of a trail. Coyotes eat holly-leaf cherry seeds, swallowing them whole. After processing through their intestinal tract the scat is deposited in an open spot away from trees and bushes in a favorable place for a holly-leaf cherry seedling.

The History of
Topanga State Park

THE INDIANS

One hundred centuries ago a small band of Indians followed a herd of deer out of Topanga Canyon onto an open slope leading to a ridge overlooking Santa Ynez Canyon. They may have been the first people to see Topanga State Park. Archaeological evidence indicates that early man could have visited the Los Angeles basin 25,000 years ago and the San Fernando Valley 9,000 years ago. The climate was cooler then and a lot wetter. The San Fernando Valley was marshy and drained by a wide Los Angeles River rather than the cement culvert that exists today.

Early man hunted the large land mammals—antelope, elk, deer, bison, and an occasional mammoth—across the broad valleys and up canyons and ridges to the hills. Camp would usually be made near the site of a kill and be changed when the food ran out.

When the last Ice Age came to an end about 11,500 years ago, southern California underwent a decisive change of climate. A lessening of moisture extending over a period of several thousand years caused the southwest to dry up and become a desert. The large mammals moved out, and eventually many of them became extinct. The Santa Monica Mountain coastal area was an attractive area for the Indians because here they continued to find food in the form of vegetation, which partially relieved the need for animals as food. When the dependence upon meat decreased, the Indians were able to remain in an area for longer periods of time so that about 7,000 years ago, permanent living sites were established on the coast. Although the people still frequently moved about in small groups, the Indians occupied the area without interruption until the Spanish invasion. This early period is identified as the Millingstone Horizon, named after the method of food preparation by which small hard seeds from sage and grasses were ground on shallow-dished stones resembling metates. Fishing and hunting were of minor importance: however, shellfish were gathered in the lagoons and along the ocean shore. Because the sea level has risen several hundred feet since the time of the original occupation, some of the artifacts are not available, the evidence being under water.

The Middle Period began about 3,800 years ago and is characterized by a greater variety of foods. A method of processing acorns to remove the tannin had been discovered which made this abundant food available for use. Deep stone mortars were employed to a great extent; fishing became important, and hunting for animals decreased. Social relationships became more complex with the increase in population. More villages were established and became relatively permanent. About 2,300 years ago during the Middle Period, a pattern of village distribution was established that remained constant until the time of the Spanish invasion.

The Late Period began about 1,500 years ago with the emergence of the Chumash culture west of the Topanga watershed, and a related culture in the Topanga area. The social structure became more complex than it was previously and more time was devoted to cultural advancements. A monetary system based on shell beads came into being about 1,300 years ago; plank canoes travelled established trade routes to the Channel Islands; fishing technology was highly developed, and a knowledge of cosmology was advanced to a point which is just now being appreciated by contemporary scholars.

At some period in time—possibly 3,000 years ago—Indians came west from the desert and displaced the Indians in the Los Angeles Basin area. This "Shoshonean Wedge," as this movement is called, extended to the ocean as far west as the ridge between Malibu Canyon and Topanga Canyon. We may speculate, then, that the first people to inhabit Topanga State Park were predecessors of the Chumash or the Yuman people and they were prehistorically displaced by Shoshonean people. We know that various dialects of Hokan (the language of the Chumash) were spoken along the coast west of Malibu. Tak'lit (the language of the Shoshoneans) was spoken east of Topanga Creek. The two distinctly different languages indicate separate origins of the people.

Metate

and

Mano

The Topanga watershed and the Santa Ynez watershed are rich in the evidence of Indian culture. More than twenty-five catalogued sites exist in upper Topanga Canyon. The old Topanga Post Office and adjacent buildings rest on an ancient Indian village, and much unreported evidence probably exists. I know of a bulldozed ridge that once held the history of the people who lived there, but bulldozing is not accepted archaeological technique, so a bit of history is lost. Plans for the Park include a resource center which will emphasize American Indian life. Interpretive facilities to show culture and ecology as well as examples of Indian structures and artisan displays should make this an important educational center.

Archaeological investigations of the first permanent inhabitants in the Topanga area show a close association with the San Dieguito culture of the same time period. Investigations of later inhabitants indicate some cultural association with the Chumash predecessors to the west. Even though territorial limits were fixed for many generations, cultural overlaps between neighboring tribes were common.

THE SPANISH

THE EXPLORERS

The California Indians' first contact with western civilization was with the Juan Rodriquez Cabrillo Expedition of 1542 on October 9th when the Spaniards anchored at Santa Monica Bay. Although in 1540 Francisco Vasquez de Coronado made a two-year exploratory trip to New Mexico, Arizona, and into Kansas looking for the "seven cities of Cibola," only stories of his trip reached the Indians of California. Sixty years after the Cabrillo expedition, Sebastian Viscaíño explored and mapped the coast of California.

THE MISSIONS

For 167 years, the Shoshonean speaking Indians and the Chumash saw no westerners until 1769 when the Gaspar de Portolá Expedition came north from Lower California to explore and colonize. After spending a few days in the Los Angeles Basin and noting that the steep cliffs along the ocean prevented coastal travel, the expedition crossed the mountains through Sepulveda Pass on 5 August, 1569. The mountains were named after Saint Monica.

The Spanish vigorously pursued their plan of a joint effort between the state and church to convert the native population into Spaniards. The church converted the Indians to Christianity and trained them as a labor force working at the missions. The state provided soldiers as protection from dissident natives as well as a means to subjugate them. San Gabriel Mission and San Fernando Mission were founded and thereby began a sequence that ultimately was fatal to the Indians. Most of the Indian villages disappeared when their members moved to the Missions to take up a new way of life.

THE MEXICANS

Mexico declared independence from Spain in 1821, forming an independent government in 1822, and an immediate shift of authority took place. The missions lost their vast land holdings and their political domination, with the final blow being struck with the secularization act of 1834. The Mexican colonization law of 1824 and the Reglamento of 1828 made land grants possible. Existing land use permits granted when Spain governed California were honored. These actions had an effect on our view of Topanga State Park History because in 1827 Xavier Alvarado and Antonio Machado were granted provisional title to Boca de Santa Monica. This grant was for Santa Monica Canyon (which runs northeast to southwest near San Vicente Blvd.) and the land west to Topanga Canyon and to the hills on the north. In 1828 Francisco Sepulveda was granted provisional title to the San Vicente Y Santa Monica Rancho which includes most of the present Topanga State Park. These two adjacent land grants are shown on the current 7½' series of topographic maps.

In 1838, Ysidro Reyes and Francisco Marquez became the new owners of Boca de Santa Monica. The following year, Sepulveda's grant was confirmed, then reconfirmed in 1846 because the title papers had been lost. In 1839, Sepulveda also claimed a large segment of his neighbors' land but lost the legal battle.

THE AMERICANS

The war between Mexico and the United States ended in 1848, and a treaty was signed guaranteeing existing property sites. In 1851, the U.S. Government established a Board of Land Commissioners to rule on the validity of claims issued under Mexican land grants. Owners of both Ranchos filed petitions in 1851 and after 30 years of delays and legal battles, United States patents were issued in 1881 to the Francisco Sepulveda family for 30,259.65 acres known as San Vicente y Santa Monica and to the Ysidro Reyes family for 6,656.93 acres known as Boca de Santa Monica. In the meantime, others had bought into the property, and subdivision activity began in 1875.

With the exception of some land on the western edge of the Park, all of the State Park land was once a part of the two Ranchos. A complete listing of intervening ownerships is not practical here, but I will discuss some of the later history that surrounds this fabulous place.

TRIPPET RANCH

Eighty acres was homesteaded in the 1890's by Mr. Joe Robison. It was bought by Cora Trippet, wife of Judge Oscar Trippet in 1917 and used primarily as a weekend retreat. The buildings that are in use today were built in the late 1930's and early '40's. The State acquired the area and has used it as the main entry to Topanga State Park.

The management objectives for the use of Trippet Ranch are to promote the rich heritage of the original occupants and to emphasize American Indian culture and ecology by the establishment of an Indian cultural center and a preserve for archaeological sites. Trippet Ranch is used as a major trailhead for hiking and is a center for natural history interpretation.

MULHOLLAND DRIVE

The northern edge of the Park is traversed by Mulholland Drive. In 1913 Bill Mulholland, Chief Engineer of the Los Angeles City Water Department proposed a road of "55 miles of scenic splendor." Work was started in the early 20's, and in October 1971, Mulholland Drive was designated a City Scenic Parkway by the Los Angeles City Council. Several trails enter the Park from Mulholland Drive.

RUSTIC CANYON

This canyon is important to the Park, but most of it belongs to the L.A. County Sanitation District and was procured in 1959 as a location for a future landfill. Several hiking trails enter the Park from the canyon. The part of the canyon a mile or two north of Sunset Blvd. includes several features of interest.

When Inceville was a prominent moving picture center, many Westerns were made in scenic Rustic Canyon. The untouched natural resource was desirable not only because it was close, but also because it lent itself to the idea of the Wild West. Later, in the 1920's, the canyon was used as an exclusive weekend residential community, and equestrians and hikers pioneered trails into the upper canyon.

In the 1930's several pieces of property were sold to individuals. One hundred acres became the home of Anatol Josepho, a

Russian refugee who came to California in 1928 and succeeded as an inventer and business man. The Josepho family lived at this retreat for a number of years, opening their home to use by servicemen during World War II. Having passed through the hands of two owners, the Josepho Ranch, in 1973, was sold to the State of California for inclusion in Topanga State Park. The fire of 1978 destroyed most of the structures, leaving the barn intact.

In 1941, Anatol Josepho bought an additional 100 acres to the north of his ranch and gave it to the Boy Scouts of America. This camp is presently used for camping and outdoor training. The fire of 1978 and several floods have caused some problems in the use of the camp. The fire burned some facilities and much of the vegetation; the winter floods periodically dump mud, sand, and rocks on the grounds — even filled the swimming pool with gravel once.

South of the Josepho Ranch is a fifty acre parcel of land originally purchased by "Jessie M. Murphy" in 1933. A large water tank, a diesel fuel tank, and a power station with generators were built even though facilities for these services were available locally. High fences and armed guards discouraged the curious. The mystery of the "Murphy" Ranch came to light when it was discovered that pro-Nazi sympathizers had been convinced by the Germanborn Herr Schmidt to finance a self-sufficient community that would be a refuge in case of war with Germany. When war broke out, Schmidt, who broadcasted to Germany over a short-wave radio set hidden on the ranch, was charged with being a Nazi spy. The fire of 1978 destroyed all but the power house.

The Huntington Hartford Foundation bought the Josepho property and the Murphy property (total of 154 acres) in 1948. The property is now public land.

SANTA MONICA FORESTRY STATION

An experimental forestry research station was established by the California State Board of Forestry in 1887. Land was donated along the eastern edge of Rustic Canyon, and by 1890 the plot had been cleared and planted. The College of Agriculture at the University of California took over the management in 1893. The project was discontinued in 1923. The site has been designated a California Historical Landmark.

WILL ROGERS HIDEAWAY

Will Rogers built a log cabin in Rustic Canyon in 1932-33 to be used as a hideaway. His daughter sold it in 1960 to Ms. Tippett, who in turn sold it to the State of California in 1966 for inclusion in Topanga State Park. A concrete dam erected about 1900 by the Santa Monica Land and Water Company is still visible in the streambed.

WILL ROGERS STATE HISTORIC PARK

This 182-acre park is adjacent to the southeast corner of Topanga State Park. Will Rogers bought the land in 1922 with the intention of building a weekend cottage where he and his family could ride horses in a rural setting. The family moved to the cabin permanently in 1928 and enlarged it to thirty-one rooms. after Will's death in 1935, his wife lived at the home until her death in 1944. Her wishes for the property and furnishings to become a memorial to her husband were carried out, and the Will Rogers estate became a State Park.

Topanga State Park was obtained incrementally by the State of California, mostly during the period 1966-73. Congressmen Teague and Alonzo Bill submitted a bill for the Federal Government to create Toyon National Urban Park. This bill died in the 1970 session of Congress. In announcing this setback for a National Park in February, 1971, Bell stated that the State of California had purchased 1,443 acres and was negotiating for more. In October of 1972, it was announced that the State was purchasing 1,700 more acres to be added to the "Santa Monica Urban Park." The purchase was made from the Garapito Creek Realty Investment Co. and the Mountain Park Realty Investment Co. for 40% of the assessed value, the difference being donated to the State by the two firms. In April 1973, Governor Ronald Reagan proposed a $91,599 increase in the State Park budget so the 4,121 acre section could be opened. In May 1973, the California Legislature passed Assemblyman Paul Priolos' bill that added 3,100 acres to the Park. Governor Reagan signed the bill, and on 1 July, 1973, the now 7,500 acre Topanga State Park was opened for public use. Subsequent additions have brought the total acreage to beyond 10,000. The acquisition of additional acreage can be expected in the future, but the Park today is already large enough to be called a major recreational area.

Environmental Hazards

Because Topanga State Park is mostly within the city limits of Los Angeles, one could expect all the conveniences of a metropolitan center, but such is not the case. Once the hiker is out of sight of the parking lot, this wild country has some unique hazards of which to be aware.

ON BECOMING LOST

One purpose of this hiking guide is to present information in such a manner that no one will become lost. Sometimes things go wrong, and a vague sense of apprehension sets in. If there is any doubt about which trail to take, it is best to stop immediately. If darkness is setting in, if one is in a hurry or very tired, then caution is most vital. This is the exact time to stop, because the temptation to plunge hopelessly forward in search of a miracle is very strong. "McAuley's Law" roughly states that "the probability of increasing the error is arithmetically proportional to the number of steps one takes after becoming confused."

After stopping and calmly thinking about the situation, mark the spot, then retrace the route to the last known point where location was certain. If this does not solve the problem, it may be necessary to return to the marked position and make scouting trips in other directions. Shout, then listen. Look at the map again. Walking downstream is not necessarily a good idea because not all canyons are passable. The middle fork of Santa Ynez Canyon presents some sheer cliffs requiring a rope rappel. Most of the gullies down East Topanga Fireroad become impassable at their lower end. Rustic Canyon is a long walk. The east fork of Rustic Canyon is a tedious fight with chaparral and some steep rock descents. Garapito Canyon and Caballero Canyon are passable, as is the west fork of Santa Ynez Canyon.

Having spent some time looking for lost trails, it is my considered opinion that only the lone hiker is in serious danger. Groups of two or more may become lost, but with mutual support they may be able to refrain from hysterically thrashing about and becoming more confused.

FIRE

Los Angeles is blessed with a capable, effective fire fighting and fire prevention department. As a result, some of the chaparral has not burned in many years and is now extremely vulnerable to intense burning. A long hot summer, followed by winds in the fall, creates a potential fire hazard. Once begun under these conditions, a rampaging fire can sweep up a slope faster than any hiker can climb out. Park personel make a daily fire danger assessment. A recorded message can be heard by dialing (213)454-2372. During periods of extreme fire danger the Park closes. This reduces the possibility of starting a fire as well as preventing danger to people in the area. Nearly all fires in the Santa Monica Mountains are caused by people.

DRINKING WATER

Some of the springs might have drinkable water, but no one knows for sure. Upstream contamination is likely, so the recommendation is to carry water or drink only from a faucet.

RAINS AND FLOODS

The annual late winter rains often present problems. Streams swell and increase the difficulty of travelling. Mud runs off the land that has been scraped by bulldozers. Firebreaks, roads and burned-over areas furnish mud to running water. Landslides occur naturally in many parts of the mountains, most of them going unnoticed because of their remoteness. Rocks rolling down into canyons are a hazard to anyone in the canyon.

SUN

The hot sun shines down on the ridge trails and reaches into the chaparral. This limits the opportunities for shade to an occasional laurel sumac tree, or the riparian woodland in a streambed. Summer sun calls for a broad brimmed hat so that both nose and ears are shaded.

Heat exhaustion and heat stroke result from the body's overheating, usually on a sunny day but not necessarily so. They are different ailments requiring separate treatment. In heat exhaustion the person feels faint and tired; his skin is moist, he may have a headache and pale skin, and could feel nauseous. The body temperature is normal, pulse is fast and feeble, and there is a possibility of cramps. Heat exhaustion happens to someone who has perspired heavily and lost body water and salts. Usually the hiker has been walking fast in warm weather without drinking enough water. To recover, the hiker should find a cool shaded place, lie down, loosen clothing, raise feet and drink fruit juice or water.

Heat stroke is possible on a hot, humid, windless day when sweat evaporation doesn't cool the body. It is identified by high body temperatures, restlessness, confusion, and sometimes unconsciousness. The skin is hot and red and may become dry. The pulse is fast and strong. Treat by getting the person to a cool place, remove the clothing, and sponge the body with lukewarm or cool water to bring the temperature down a few degrees. The condition is serious—get medical help.

TICKS

Ticks are found on branches of brush and blades of grass, especially in the spring. Actually, one hardly ever finds a tick except on a hiker. To remove a tick grasp it gently but firmly between a finger and thumb, and pull slowly until it gives. Some people prefer to use tweezers or tissue, but the result should be the same. Apply some type of antiseptic to the wound. Once a tick is firmly attached and begins to swell, removal becomes difficult. I recommend placing lotion or oil on the tick, wait about ten minutes then remove with a steady pull. If the head fails to come out, it will probably become infected in a couple of days, and then come out on its own. See a physician if you become ill after a bite. I have not heard of "tick fever" in the Santa Monicas but the possibility exists. Lyme disease is transmitted to animals by ticks. Animals then, in turn, infect ticks. I have not heard of a verified

Lyme disease case in the Santa Monica Mountains. The entire area is subject to the disease because an infected dog or person from an infected area outside the Santa Monica Mountains could introduce the disease locally.

This tick was waiting to drop onto a warm body.

INSECTS

The usual flies, mosquitoes and other bothersome insects live in the Park but are not as evident as in damper climates. They have never given me much concern.

Hollow logs support colonies of bees in a few places. They have never given me any trouble, but then I don't go around thumping hollow logs to see what happens.

Some people are allergic to the bite of the cone-nose bug. The den of the dusky-footed woodrat is likely to harbor the cone-nose bug, so avoid the encounter by not poking around any large pile of sticks and twigs.

REPTILES

Rattlesnakes are the only dangerous reptiles in the Park, and they are dangerous only when threatened. A hiker should look where he steps, avoiding deep grass and hidden rock ledges. Give snakes a chance to avoid you, and avoid them.

PLANT LIFE

Contact with poison oak causes an allergic reaction and produces a severe rash on most people. The three-leaf formations are identifiable during the growing season. In the fall the leaves turn red and drop off, but the bare branches are still toxic.

Some poisonous plants that grow in the Park can cause serious problems if eaten.

Poison oak
Three ovate lobed leaflets constitute each leaf. The two-inch leaves are shiny green on top, turn red and drop in the Fall. Small greenish-white flowers are borne in a drooping panicle.

Trail System

A network of fireroads and trail provides routes for movement within the Park. All travel must be done on foot, horseback, or non-motorized vehicle. Dogs are not allowed in the Park.

The varieties of scenery and hiking terrain are almost without limit. Some level trails with good footing make for introductory walks, and steep climbs with considerable elevation gain are a challenge to the experienced hiker.

Highways and roads provide some access to the south, west and north sides of the Park. East entry is accomplished by trail. The numbers on the map correspond to the trailhead numbers.

The following ten pages show the major trailheads used by hikers, bikers, and equestrians. The numbers on the facing maps correlate with the numbered paragraphs. The fold-out map in the pocket on the inside of the back cover is consistent with these numbers.

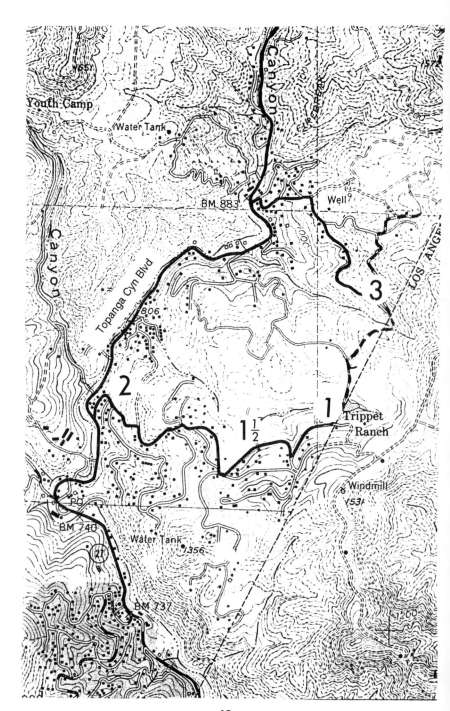

#1 TRIPPET RANCH ENTRANCE

Go east on Entrada Road from State Hwy 27 (Topanga Canyon Blvd) just north of the town of Topanga. Once on Entrada Road, turn left at every street intersection, and go 1.1 miles to the Park entrance. There is a parking lot inside the gate. Parking fee required. Trippet Ranch is the Park Headquarters and center of information. Restroom, picnic area, pay phone and information available.

#1-1/2

One-fourth mile west of Trippet Ranch on Entrada Road a trail goes north into the Park.

#2 DEAD HORSE ENTRANCE

Go east on Entrada Road from State Highway 27 for about 200 yards, turning left onto a flat, paved parking area. The lot is closed at night. Parking is free at present. A restroom is available.

#3 HILLSIDE DRIVE ENTRANCE

Go east on Hillside Drive from State Highway 27 about 1½ miles north of the town of Topanga. Hillside Drive makes a 90° right turn after a short steep climb, and continues to twist and turn until reaching a gate .7 miles from Hwy 27. Parking space is at a premium, and there could be difficulty in turning around. The old road beyond the gate intersects the Musch Ranch Trail. Not recommended for use.

#4 COMMUNITY HOUSE ENTRANCE

About 1.9 miles north of the town of Topanga on Highway 27, a road on the east leads uphill about 1/4 mile to the Community House. Several parking lots are near the building. A trail begins on the ridge east of the building and goes uphill. It is now overgrown and could present a route-finding challenge. This entrance has not received much use and is not recommended.

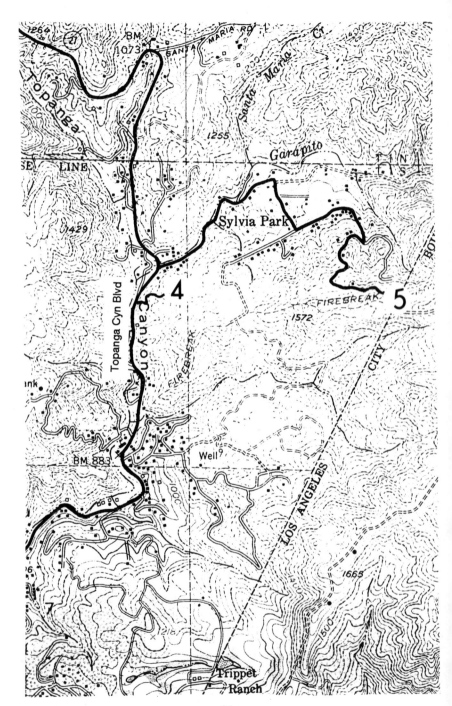

#5   CHENEY DRIVE ENTRANCE

Two miles north of the town of Topanga on Highway 27, go east on Cheney Drive.   Make a right turn at about 1/2 mile; turn left on Callon Drive, then a sharp right on Penny Drive, following it as it makes several turns mostly left.   The upper end of this road is privately maintained and on private property so I recommend against its use.

#6   TOPANGA CREEK

A corner of Topanga State Park is visited daily by more people than all the rest of the Park areas combined—and most of these visitors are not aware that they are in the Park.   2.7 miles north of the Pacific Coast Highway on Hwy 27 a sign proclaims the entrance to the city of Los Angeles.   .9 of a mile further on, the road leaves the city limits. This .9 of a mile area is also Park property, including the canyon and the magnificent cliffs to the east.

Parking is not allowed along the highway, so access to foot travel is difficult.   Just upstream from the bridge (two miles from the Pacific Coast Highway) is a parking area that will hold about ten cars.   No trail enters the area.   Walk upstream, sometimes climbing over boulders.   You will find this to be a riparian paradise; bay trees, big-leaf maples, willows, and many water-loving flowers.   "Purple Stones" is a not too well known climbing area near the creek bed.   Several large boulders with some difficult routes in the 5.10 range are shaded by trees. These are short pitches but challenging.

#7 FIREROAD 30 ENTRANCE

In Woodland Hills, go east on Mulholland Drive from Highway 27. Mulholland Drive enters the Park (no sign) at about 3.8 miles. At 4.0 miles, a metal gate on the south marks the beginning of Fireroad 30, which leads into the northern end of the Park.

#8 BENT ARROW ENTRANCE

In Woodland Hills, go 4.8 miles east on Mulholland Drive from Hwy 27. The entrance to the Bent Arrow Trail is on the right, close to the base of the hill. There is limited parking space off the road.

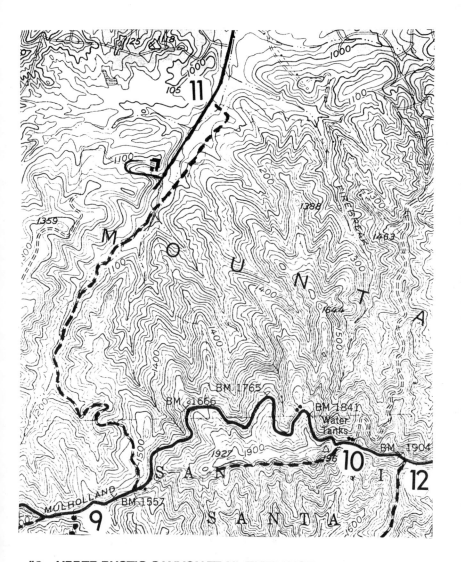

#9 UPPER RUSTIC CANYON TRAIL ENTRANCE

Two hundred yards east of the Bent Arrow Trail Entrance (#8), Rustic Canyon goes downhill to the south from Mulholland Dr. This trail leaves the Park and enters Rustic Canyon, which is owned by the Department of Sanitation. Public use of this area is on the same basis as Park use. Trails out of Rustic Canyon lead up onto Rogers Ridge and back into the Park.

#10 FIREROAD 27-A ENTRANCE

Six and three tenths miles from Highway 27 on Mulholland Drive a large parking lot on the south side is at the entrance to Fireroad 27-A. The fireroad leads to the east end of the Bent Arrow Trail and to the trail into Rustic Canyon. No facilities. (Map on previous page.)

#11 CABALLERO TRAILHEAD

In Tarzana, drive south of the Ventura Freeway on Reseda Blvd. Four routes lead into the Park from this major entrance from the San Fernando Valley. No facilities. (Map on previous page.)

#12 SULLIVAN RIDGE WEST (FIREROAD 26) ENTRANCE

Six and six-tenths miles from Highway 27 on Mulholland Drive, Fireroad 26 starts its run to the south along the ridge. The road is on Department of Sanitation property, and at present no trails lead west into Upper Rustic Canyon.

Near the southern end of the fireroad, a private road leads down to the Boy Scout Camp Josepho. There is also a bushwhack route for the adventurous. Two routes lead east into Sullivan Canyon, one at the north end of Fireroad 26, the other near the south end. No facilities (Map on previous page.)

#13 SULLIVAN CANYON ENTRANCE

Drive 6.2 miles east of the Pacific Coast Highway on Sunset Blvd. and turn north onto Mandeville Canyon Road. Turn left on Westridge Road and follow it as it twists and turns for 1.1 mile to reach Bayliss Road. Make another left turn, then go 0.3 mile to Queensferry Road, turn left and park.

#14 SULLIVAN RIDGE WEST, PACIFIC PALISADES ENTRANCE

Four and seven-tenths miles from the Pacific Coast Highway on Sunset Blvd. turn north on Amalfi Dr. and follow it to Capri Dr. Turn Left on Capri. This trailhead is difficult to use if you go in by car; the road beyond Amalfi is narrow, there is no good turnaround place, and at best, parking room for only 2 cars. I recommend that any travel on Capri be by foot or bicycle.

#15 WILL ROGERS STATE HISTORIC PARK

Drive east on Sunset Blvd 3.9 miles from the Pacific Coast Hwy to the Will Rogers State Park Road, and into the Park. A fee is charged for parking. Facilities include restrooms, picnic area, information, guided tours, and a polo field.

#16 TEMESCAL CANYON ROAD TRAILHEAD

Drive east on Sunset Blvd. 2.5 miles from the Pacific Coast Hwy to Temescal Cyn Rd; turn north and park at the Conference Center. Sign in and out at the information booth.

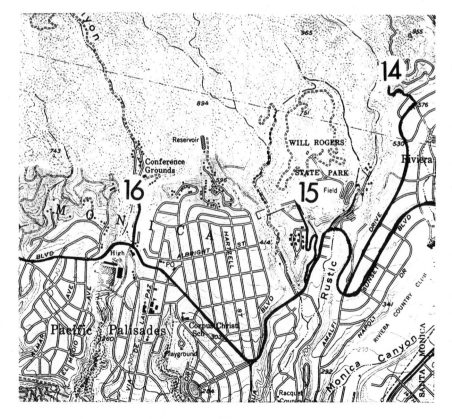

#18   SANTA YNEZ CANYON PARK TRAILHEAD

Go east .5 mile on Sunset Blvd. from the Pacific Coast Hwy, and turn north (left) on Palisades Drive. One and 3/4 miles from Sunset Blvd., a sign on the left identifies Santa Ynez Canyon Park. Park outside and walk in.

#19   PALISADES HIGHLANDS TRAILHEAD

The Santa Ynez Canyon Trail goes through a tunnel under Vereda de la Montura about 1/2 mile upstream from entry #18. Park along the street and find the trail as it comes through the north end of the tunnel on the east side of the stream.

#20   TRAILER CANYON TRAILHEAD

Drive north on Palisades Drive, turning left on Palisades Court, and left onto Michael Lane. The trailhead is on the east side, about 200 yards from Palisades Court, near a small flood control basin.

#21   PASEO MIRAMAR ENTRANCE

Drive east .3 mile on Sunset Blvd. from the Pacific Coast Hwy to Paseo Miramar and turn north (left). Park at the far end of Paseo Miramar Avenue. Limited street parking is available.

#22   LOS LIONES ENTRANCE

Drive east .3 mile on Sunset Blvd. from the Pacific Coast Hwy to Los Liones Drive and turn left. Park on the Drive, but avoid the church parking lot.

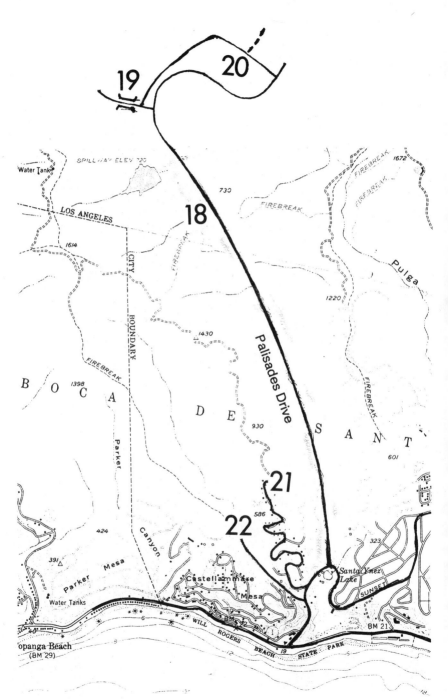

Recommended Hikes

Some hikes have become popular and are worth describing in more detail. These recommended hikes will give you an overall view of the Park and an insight to the trail system. The description of each hike gives the distance in miles, the elevation gain and loss, the type of terrain, the walking time and the starting point. People walk at different speeds and do not react the same to steep hills so you may find some variation in the times listed. The times shown are the actual time that it took me, modified by time-outs for picture-taking or investigating some subject of local interest to me. I walk nearly 3 mph and need an additional 1/2 hour for every 1,000 feet of elevation gain. Boulder hopping or other difficult trail conditions slow me down. I walk faster on cool mornings than I do on hot afternoons, so expect some discrepancies.

When hiking out of Trippet Ranch familiarize yourself with the features. A wealth of information is available from the Rangers on duty, and Park Docents are often available to answer questions and lead scheduled walks. A native plant garden is located west of the parking lot and a self-guided nature trail starts at a point near the pond. Don't overlook these benefits.

Index of Hikes

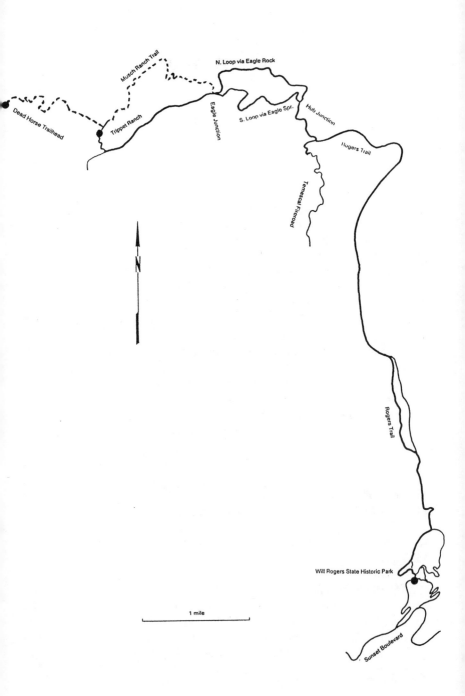

Musch Ranch Trail

N. Loop via Eagle Rock

Dead Horse Trailhead

Trippet Ranch

Eagle Junction

S. Loop via Eagle Spr.

Hub Junction

Rogers Trail

Temescal Fireroad

N

Rogers Trail

Will Rogers State Historic Park

1 mile

Sunset Boulevard

Distance:	11.45 miles via Musch Ranch
	10.95 miles via The Latitude
	(one way)
Elevation:	1200' gain, 2000' loss
Terrain:	Trail and fireroad
Time:	5½ hours eastbound
	Slightly more westbound
Trailhead:	Dead Horse Trailhead (#2)

The Backbone Trail is a 65 mile east-west route through the mountains. Parts of the trail west of here are incomplete. In Topanga State Park we can walk 11½ miles of backcountry on the trail in near isolation.

This description of the trail is west to east, from Topanga State Park to Will Rogers State Historic Park, as a one-way trip. It is necessary for you to arrange transportation for a car shuttle. You may want to walk this trail each way to get the best perspective. Hike #2 describes this walk east to west. One day I walked from WRSHP to Trippet Ranch and back. It was a long day for me.

Find the Dead Horse trailhead by driving 1/2 mile north of the Topanga Post Office on Highway 27 (Topanga Canyon Boulevard). Turn east onto Entrada Road on a steep uphill curve. Almost immediately turn left on a blind curve into a paved parking lot. Facilities include a rest room. The lot closes at night. No parking fee is required (as of 1991).

Leave the parking lot on the east side and go uphill. The one and a quarter mile of the Dead Horse Trail segment starts through chaparral. The route then goes into riparian woodland and, more chaparral, then enters an oak woodland at the edge of grassland.

About one-half hour after beginning the hike you will reach a road. A right turn takes you across the earthen dam by the pond, to the Trippet Ranch parking lot. A left turn at the road takes you onto the Musch Ranch Trail. Either route will take you to Eagle Junction where the routes join. I'll describe the Musch Ranch segment now, and the Fireroad segment via The Latitude on a later hike (#3, Eagle Spring Loop).

Upon reaching the road at the end of the Dead Horse Trail turn left and walk about 100 yards. Watch for the trail on the right that angles across a grass field. The Musch Ranch Trail quickly enters an enchanting glen of riparian woodland of oak, laurel and sycamore trees. After winding through the densely wooded area the trail comes out for a short glimpse of chaparral. It then dips back into a ravine cool enough to support ferns and other streamside plants.

The trail continues uphill and into chaparral. About one mile along the Musch Ranch Trail you will come to an overnight camping ground in a stand of eucalyptus trees. Facilities include restrooms, drinking water, picnic tables and horse corrals. No fires allowed.

One hundred yards beyond the campground the trail turns left as it crosses a dry streambed then gently climbs a grassy slope. Angle right to continue uphill. A side trail branches left to go north into a grassland but you will want to stay on the main trail. Following this trail you will alternate going across grasslands (usually dominated by black mustard) and into riparian woodlands where the trail crosses streams. After crossing the fourth stream prepare yourself for an abrupt uphill climb where you will gain 350' in three-quarters of a mile. Upon reaching the fireroad at Eagle Junction, two routes become available. The lefthand route takes you uphill immediately and passes Eagle Rock, then the Garapito Trail junction. The righthand route goes slightly downhill for awhile, passes the side trail to Eagle Spring, and makes a 400 foot gain to the Hub. Both routes are 1.4 miles long and meet at the Hub. Take your choice.

Four roads intersect at the Hub. The High Trail and the Low Trail come in from the west. North on Fireroad 30 goes 2 miles and ends at Mulholland Drive. Today's hike takes you to the south on Fireroad 30 (Temescal Fireroad). A portable toilet at the Hub is your last opportunity until reaching Will Rogers State Historic Park. As you travel south, Cathedral Rock will be on your left. A steep, gravelly trail leads up and into the "cathedral." Isolated inside and protected from wind, I like it as a lunch stop.

About 1/2 mile farther south on a level fireroad turn left onto Rogers Ridge Trail. You have 6.3 miles to go—mostly downhill. We have come 5.3 miles. As we walk east, Rustic Canyon is on the left and soon the head of Temescal Canyon comes into view on the right. The Bay Tree Trail branches left at this point and drops down to the floor of Rustic Canyon. The Backbone Trail keeps to the ridges for most of the hike. About one mile after leaving Temescal Fireroad, a 90° right turn puts you on a southerly heading and a downhill grade. You might want to stop here to tighten the laces on your boots because a lot of downhill can otherwise cause toe problems.

The mileage chart (pages 58 - 59) shows approximate mileages at recognizable points. Look on the right for a trail to Peak 1756'. At a right bend in the trail you will pass the best shade, a multi-trunked coast live oak. Another mile brings you to a saddle on the ridge and a trail fork that leads to the bottom of Rustic Canyon and an alternate route to WRSHP. When you cross Chicken Ridge Bridge less than 1½ miles of hiking remains. Great views of the ocean and the sprawling metropolitan area have been developing as the hike progresses. I have my favorite viewing points but you might want to pick your own. Being aware that the parks close at night and parking gets complicated, I must state that a night view of the city from this trail will long be remembered.

When you reach the dirt road at Will Rogers State Historic Park several routes are available. All lead to the visitor's center and parking lot.

Complete your car shuttle.

Los Angeles from Rogers Ridge

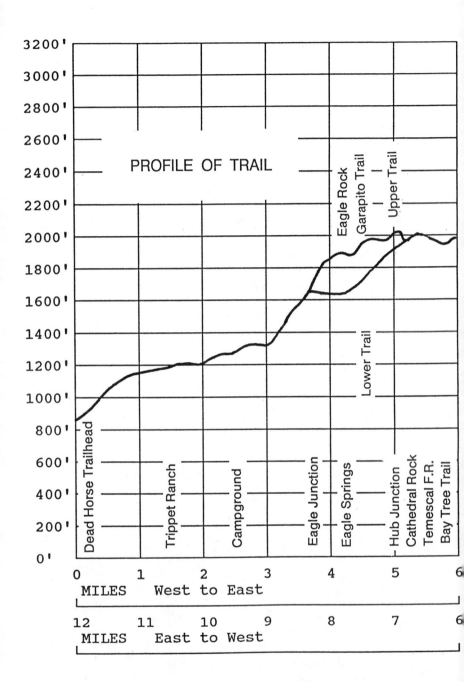

PROFILE OF TRAIL

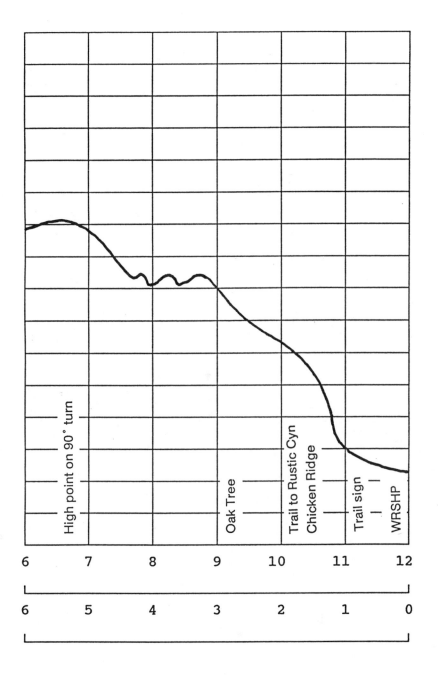

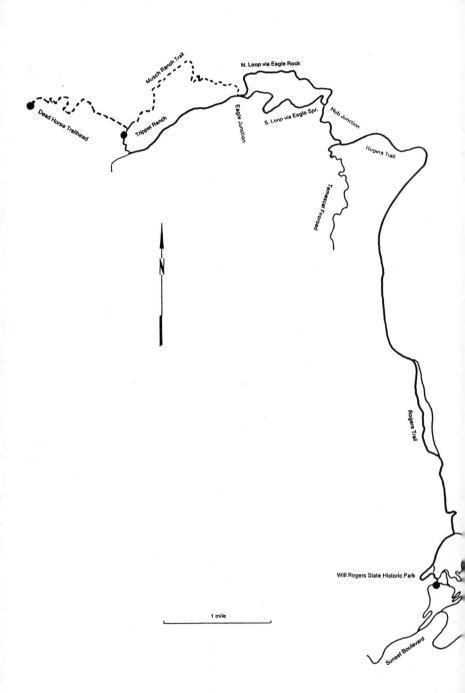

Musch Ranch Trail

N. Loop via Eagle Rock

Dead Horse Trailhead

Trippet Ranch

Eagle Junction

S. Loop via Eagle Spr.

Hub Junction

Rogers Trail

Temescal Fireroad

N

Rogers Trail

Will Rogers State Historic Park

1 mile

Sunset Boulevard

HIKE 2

Distance:	11.45 miles via Musch Ranch
	10.95 miles via The Latitude
Elevation:	2000' gain, 1200' loss
Terrain:	Trail and fireroad
Time:	5½ hours
Trailhead:	Will Rogers State Historic Park (#15)

The Backbone Trail is an equestrian and hiking trail from Will Rogers State Historic Park to Point Mugu State Park. It is not complete because some of the proposed trail route is privately owned; however, the section described here is on public land and is in use. Hike #1 describes this walk west to east.

The hike begins at Will Rogers State Historic Park which adjoins Topanga State Park. Start near the tennis courts west of Park Headquarters. Several trails are available and it's hard to go wrong. Because a gentle warm-up prepares one for a long day, I recommend that after an initial steep uphill by trail you turn left when reaching the fireroad. A sign here shows .7 miles to Inspiration Point. This trail maintains a gradual climb and circles onto a small ridge near Inspiration Point. The next fork on the left leads to the route uphill to the north on Rogers Ridge. The impression that this trail is in a hurry to justify its name "Backbone" is soon realized. A steep climb on a rocky trail quickly upholds the name. Thirty steady minutes of walking puts you high on the ridge but still only 3 airmiles from the ocean. The view of the shoreline, curving to form Santa Monica Bay then going west, is most impressive. Rivas Canyon on the west is short and steep and will be in view for less than 2 miles as the Backbone Trail bears northwest. Rustic Canyon on the east is much larger and quite impressive—it will be to the right of the hiking route for most of the way. You will cross Chicken Ridge bridge. Once the trail went across a knife edge, adding some excitement, but the bridge is a comfort. The trail becomes comfortable on top of Rogers Ridge with some moderate downhill and uphill stretches as it leads from one little peak to

Chicken Ridge Bridge from the trail above.
Santa Monica Bay in the background.

another. At a saddle, a side trail cuts back to the right and goes to the floor of Rustic Canyon. The Backbone Trail branches left and drops a short distance into Rivas Canyon to follow the old road up to the head of the canyon. As an alternate route you could stay on the Old Rogers Ridge trail—both trails join again at the saddle. Although the ridge trail is at times overgrown, it offers a more commanding view than the lower trail. This entire area was burned during the 1978 Mandeville fire, and whatever shade that chaparral offers is gone. The first good resting spot is in the shade of a four-trunked coast live oak east of Peak 1756. The oak is on the saddle at the head of Rivas Canyon, about 1 hour from the start of the hike. Shade is hard to find.

The trail climbs west for a few hundred yards before resuming a northwest course. Temescal Canyon comes into view on the left, presenting a close-up of a unique natural area. Temescal Canyon along with Rustic and Sullivan Canyons, provides a large, undeveloped area of pristine plant communities that have not been disturbed.

The outhouse at the Hub. This is your only chance between WRSHP and Musch Ranch.

Glimpses of Fireroad 30 come into view across Temescal Canyon to to the west. Fireroad 26 to the east runs along Sullivan Ridge West and is also in view. After a respite of level walking and even some downhill interspersed with some uphill, the trail climbs steadily for about 3/4 mile. You gain 300' and reach Peak 2042 at the headwaters of Temescal Canyon. The trail makes an abrupt turn to the left and goes west 1 mile where it intersects Fireroad 30. Temescal Peak south of the junction is the highest point in the Park at 2126'. It can easily be climbed by using a firebreak that begins about 100 yards south of Fireroad 30. Not only does Temescal Peak offer a good view, it also has the distinction of being the apex of three watersheds: Temescal Canyon to the east; Rustic Canyon to the northeast; and Santa Ynez Canyon to the west.

The Backbone Trail continues north on Fireroad 30 for less than 1/2 mile before coming to Hub Junction, a 4-road intersection. On the right, before reaching Hub Junction, Cathedral Rock offers a rest, lunch stop, or just a beautiful rocky crag to climb on. When we reach Hub Junction, three roads are available. The one on the right goes downhill and eventually reaches Mulholland Drive. The one on the left goes downhill to Eagle Spring. The middle road goes uphill and can be used as an alternate route. It leads to the back side of Eagle Rock where a side trail leads to the top for a spectacular view of Santa Ynez Canyon. The road visible below passes Eagle Spring which can be identified by the remains of wooden water tanks. The upper trail continues on the road going steeply downhill to Eagle Junction. Although Eagle Rock is a massive sandstone outcropping, an intrusion of volcanic rock dominates the area to the southwest and is visible along the road. A close inspection shows brownish-rust-colored "onion rocks" in the roadcut. Weathering and the release of internal pressure causes this unusual looking rock formation.

The lower trail passes Eagle Spring with its benefits of shade and the spring. A slight uphill grade beyond Eagle Spring reminds you of your leg muscles.

Two trail choices are available at Eagle Junction. A continuation of the fireroad southwest brings you to The "Latitude" and a road junction where a right turn takes you to Trippet Ranch in 1½ miles. A right turn at Eagle Junction puts you on the Musch Ranch Trail and leads you to Trippet Ranch in 2.2 miles.

Facilities at Trippet Ranch include a pay phone, a ranger,

picnic tables, drinking water and restrooms. From this point to the end of the hike is 1¼ miles, mostly downhill.

Leave the Trippet parking lot from the north end, cross the dam and turn left onto the Deadhorse Trail. A grassland is on your right and oak woodland to the left. When the trail starts down through chaparral keep an eye out for a trail branching right—take it. The normal tendency is to continue straight ahead and become temporarily lost. After turning right you will continue through a chamise dominated chaparral plant community. As you lose elevation, and as the stream nears, the plant community changes to a riparian woodland with sycamore and bay trees. Cross the creek on a rustic bridge and within minutes you are at the parking lot.

The Backbone Trail temporarily stops here. Although not actually in Topanga State Park, land for the trail is in public ownership. Eventually the trail will go west to connect with the existing Saddle Peak segment at the top of Stunt Road.

Bridge on the Dead Horse Trail

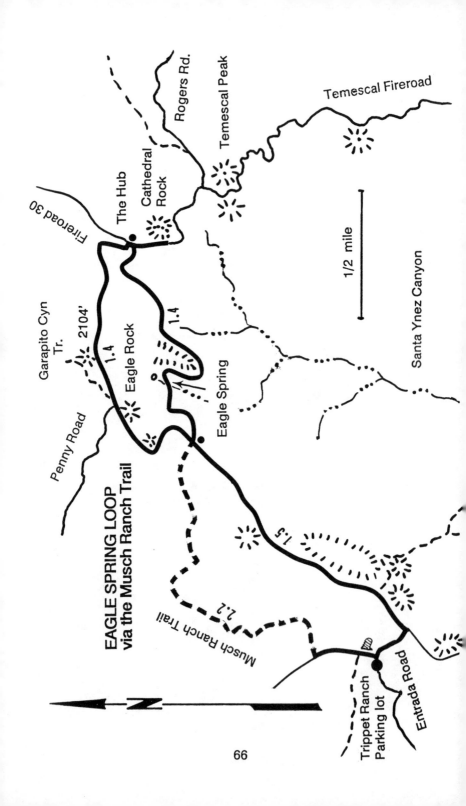

**EAGLE SPRING LOOP
via the Musch Ranch Trail**

Rogers Rd.

Temescal Peak

Temescal Fireroad

Cathedral Rock

The Hub

Fireroad 30

1/2 mile

Santa Ynez Canyon

Garapito Cyn Tr.

2104'

Eagle Rock

1.4

1.4

Penny Road

Eagle Spring

1.5

Musch Ranch Trail

2.2

Trippet Ranch Parking lot

Entrada Road

66

HIKE 3

Distance:	7 miles roundtrip
Elevation:	900' gain and loss
Terrain:	Fireroad and trail
Time:	2-3/4 hours
Trailhead:	Trippet Ranch (#1)

Eagle Spring Loop takes you on a trip to some spectacular features of the Park. The variety includes secluded glens, a high ridge, a spring, and a view from the top of Eagle Rock.

The Musch Ranch Trail begins near Trippet Ranch and ends high on a ridge at Eagle Junction. Start the hike at the picnic grounds near the pond and go north on the macadam road for a hundred yards. Watch for the trail on the right that angles across the grass field. The Musch Ranch Trail quickly enters an enchanting glen of riparian woodland of oak, laurel and sycamore trees. After winding through the densely wooded area the trail comes out for a short glimpse of chaparral. It then dips back into a ravine cool enough to support ferns and other streamside plants.

The trail goes uphill and into the chaparral. About 3/4 mile from the parking lot it passes a stand of eucalyptus trees below the Musch Ranch. Two hundred yards beyond the eucalyptus trees the trail turns left as it crosses a dry streambed then gently climbs a grassy slope and comes to a trail junction. Turn right (the left trail goes to trailhead #4), leading down into an oak woodland and another stream crossing. Soon you will find that after climbing east on a grassy ridge another fork in the trail appears—turn left. The trail to the ridge is steep and tedious, but the view from on top is worth the effort. Upon reaching the fireroad, turn left and continue uphill.

Eagle Rock is a massive monolith of stone overlooking the head of Santa Ynez Canyon. Hundreds of caves, carved during thousands of years of water erosion, are recessed in the cliff. The first view of the rock comes into sight very suddenly on the right, as the fireroad makes a climbing turn left. Take a timely stop—not just to rest after the 700' climb from the Musch Ranch—but to feel the majesty of this stately crag.

The road continues uphill for about 1/4 mile at which point a trail on the right leads to the top of Eagle Rock. The walk to the top of the rock is short and steep, requiring non-slip footgear for safety. In the top of the rock is a cave from which one can see a vista of the canyon.

Hikers climb the back side of Eagle Rock

The road runs east on the top of the ridge for another mile. Garapito Canyon on the north drains into Topanga Canyon. Santa Ynez Canyon on the south drains into the Pacific Ocean near Sunset Blvd.· Both canyons present views of virgin chaparral. At the east end of the ridge, the road joins three others at Hub Junction. Fireroad 30 on the left tops the ridge that meets Mulholland Drive 2 miles to the north. The south continuation of Fireroad 30 (named Temescal Fireroad from this point and south) runs along the crest for 5 miles before dropping down into Temescal Canyon near Sunset Boulevard. The road on the immediate right goes to Eagle Spring and is the return route of this hike.

If time permits or if a lunch stop is in order, take a short side trip to Cathedral Rock, three hundred yards south of the "Hub" along Temescal Fireroad. The easiest entry is beyond the rock at a break in the laurel sumac where a steep clearing leads north to a notch through the sandstone crest. The sheltered recess within the protective walls has room for at least 25 people to sit on rocks or the grass.

Upon returning to the "Hub," turn left, walking an easy down-hill grade to Eagle Spring. Eagle Spring quietly originates as seepage out of the sandstone rock in upper Santa Ynez Canyon. A small dammed up pool of water feeds into a pipe that runs under the streambed a couple hundred yards to fill a large wooden tank. Two tanks have fallen apart. A beautiful stand of poison oak grows between the tank and the stream. (Beautiful may not be descriptive, depending on one's view of poison oak.) Oaks and sycamores line the stream, contrasting with the chaparral that dominates the terrain.

Only one of these tanks remains at Eagle Spring.

Chamise is an important chaparral shrub. It root-crown sprouts after a fire and stabilizes steep hillsides.

This can be noted along the upper road.

Continue west on the road, and Eagle Rock comes into sight on the right. This may be the most imposing view because Eagle Rock is above, towering over all that it surveys. A side trail goes to the base but expect the footing to be poor and to find brush reaching across in places because the trail isn't graded or maintained. The road makes a sweeping left turn as it gains altitude climbing to a saddle on the ridge, meeting the north half of the Eagle Spring loop road. This is also the junction with the Musch Ranch Trail.

Rather than taking the Musch Ranch Trail back to Trippet Ranch, stay on the road as it heads southwest. Trippet Ranch can be seen down the hill in an oak woodland. Just before the road enters the wooded area, a trail from Santa Ynez Canyon comes in on the left. A few hundred yards farther on, a road intersects on the right leading to Trippet Ranch and the end of the hike.

PROFILE OF TRAIL

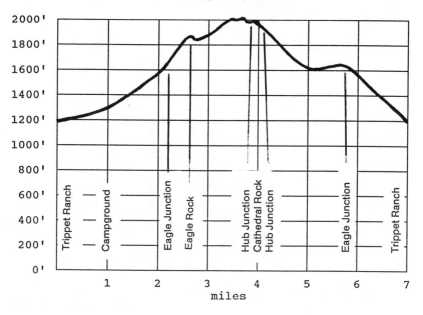

Big pod ceanothus is the dominant plant of the chaparral along the lower road.

71

HIKE 4

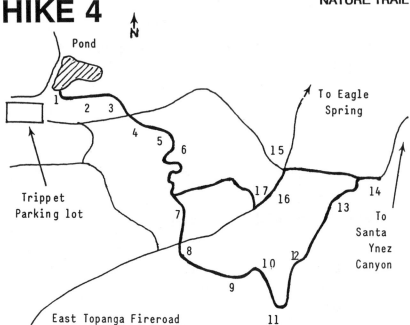

The Nature Trail is a one-mile, self-guided walk from the picnic area near the pond at Trippet Ranch.

Begin walking in an oak woodland, passing through open grassland, then after a gentle climb through more oak woodland, come out onto a chaparral-covered slope overlooking Santa Ynez Canyon and a view of the ocean.

A box containing brochures is located at station #1. In the event that the demand for brochures exceeds the supply, use this abbreviated description of the features at each station.

(This description of the Nature Trail has been condensed from the text prepared by the Topanga State Park Docents.)

1. **Pond.** Water attracts animals and birds.

2. **Poison Oak.** This 3-leaved plant causes a rash.

3. **Squirrel tree.** The burrow at the base of the tree is the home of a California Ground Squirrel.

4. **Gopher holes.** The mounds of loose dirt cover the home and feeding tunnels of Botta's Pocket Gopher.

5. **Fallen tree.**   The Trippet fire of 1973 burned this tree, but it is still alive.

6. **Oak woodland.**   The dense canopy of the Coast live oaks creates a relatively cool and moist climate for the plants and animals which live in its shade.

7. **Grassland.**   Grass and wildflowers come to life with winter rains and spring warmth.   Moisture disappears from the soil with the first heat of summer, and the grassland turns brown.

8. **Animal tracks.**   This sandy area in the fireroad often holds-the-record that animals have walked here.

9. **Ocean view.**   Facing south you can see the ocean and feel a cool, moist onshore breeze.

10. **Chaparral.**   The thin rocky soil on this slope supports chaparral growth.

11. **Canyon view.**   Santa Ynez Canyon drains water from the hills, forming a stream that flows to the ocean.

12. **Water savers.**   Chaparral shrubs have adapted in many ways to reduce the amount of water lost through their leaves.   Notice these water-saving characteristics: small size, waxy coating, light color (especially underside), folded or curled, and covered with hairs.

13. **Chaparral fire.**   The Topanga Canyon fire of 1977 burned everything above ground.   That was the beginning of a new cycle of life in the chaparral community that can be seen today.

14. **Sandstone cliffs.**   Rocks of the Topanga Formation consist of grains of sand cemented together to form hard sandstone.

15. **Mountain tops.**   Looking north and west, notice that the tops of the mountains are all roughly the same height.   These mountain tops were once below sea level before the whole area was uplifted.

16. **Volcanic rock.**   Widespread volcanic activity intruded into the sandstone while it was still under the ocean.   The fine-grained rock in this roadcut is a volcanic rock called basalt.

17. **Inside a flower.**   The wildflowers along the path support a wide variety of insects.

HIKE 5

EAST TOPANGA FIREROAD
to the Overlook
Roundtrip from Trippet Ranch

Distance:	6 miles
Elevation:	1500' gain and loss
Terrain:	Fireroad
Time:	2-3/4 hours
Trailhead:	Trippet Ranch (#1)

The crest of the ridge dividing Topanga Canyon and Santa Ynez Canyon offers spectacular views of canyons, ridges, and the Pacific Ocean. Plan on 2-3/4 hours to walk 6 miles roundtrip on a dirt and gravel fireroad. You will gain 1500' in several stretches with some nearly level walking in between, making it less effort than if done all at once. Chaparral dominates the plant life along the route except for the oak woodland near Trippet Ranch. A wide variety of spring wildflowers grows along the route, and good exposures of the geological features are prominent.

Begin the hike at the Trippet Ranch parking lot by going uphill in a southerly direction. The dirt road crosses a small sloping meadow and then enters an oak grove before cresting on the saddle of the ridge. Here where the road intersects with another, turn right onto the East Topanga Fireroad, which heads southwest in a gentle climb through an extensive grove of Coast live oaks. After a wide sweeping left turn, the trail reaches a high point and goes downhill.

The rock underfoot changes from sandstone to basalt as the road starts down. A water tank built in 1978 is hidden in a rock opening on the left. For the remainder of the hike, the route goes in a southerly direction with many turns which conform with the contour of the ridge.

West of the ridge, and about 1,000 feet below, Topanga Creek cuts a canyon through the mountains. Periodically the heavy winter rains cause flooding in the canyon. The flooding early in 1980 washed out several homes, the water system, and sections of the highway.

Although the creek in Santa Ynez Canyon on the east drains a smaller watershed than Topanga Canyon, it cuts an equally impressive network of ravines. Massive slabs of tilted sandstone form one bank of the stream in mid-canyon. The other bank is a rock cliff dotted with some caves.

Up on the ridge we pass a cliff on our left. The reddish rock including cobbles is a non-marine Oligocene sequence formed about 35 million years ago when the land was an immense flood plain. Forty-five minutes after starting the hike, begin looking for a firebreak that angles off to the right. The firebreak runs on the crest of a north-south ridge that peaks out on a knoll called "The Overlook." The Pacific Ocean sprawls out to the south; on a clear day the Palos Verdes Penninsula and Santa Catalina Island are visible. The top of The Overlook has been bulldozed clean, but an impenetrable stand of chaparral starts at the fringe and continues down the slope. This is a popular place for the turn-around of the hike.

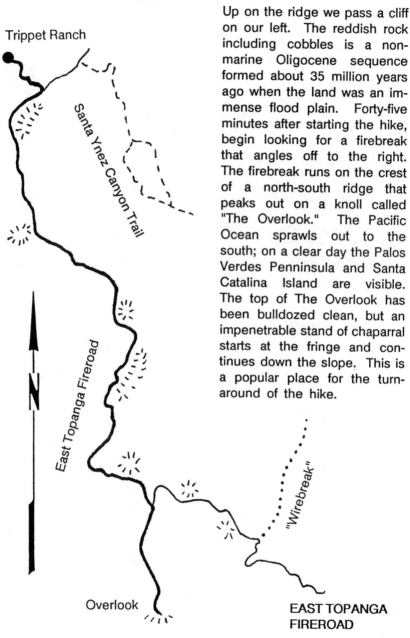

Trippet Ranch

Santa Ynez Canyon Trail

East Topanga Fireroad

N

"Wirebreak"

Overlook

EAST TOPANGA FIREROAD

Santa Monica Bay from the East Topanga Fireroad. (Note the "Wirebreak" coming from lower left to upper right.)

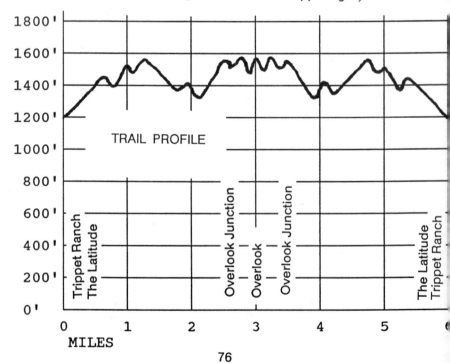

TRAIL PROFILE

Once a year a group of us do the "Lemming Hike." The serious part is downhill bushwhack between the Overlook and the ocean. Do not try this on your own. It is easy to get into trouble on this particular chaparral slope. A strong hiking group with a lot of detailed route instruction will still have a miserable but exhilarating hike. For a detailed explanation read the route instructions in *Hiking Trails of the Santa Monica Mountains.* Then put on your goggles, gloves, and long sleeves.

The end of the "Lemming Hike" at Topanga Beach

HIKE 6

Distance: 5 miles roundtrip
Elevation: 1000' gain and loss
Terrain: Fireroad
Time: 2¼ hours
Trailhead: Paseo Miramar (#21)

East Topanga Fireroad climbs northwest along the ridge between Santa Ynez Canyon and Los Liones Canyon. This hike offers spectacular views of the Pacific, the largest ocean in the world, and of a substantial urban area—the Los Angeles basin. The hike description takes advantage of the elevation and the view points along the trail. The fireroad goes to Trippet Ranch and beyond but the turnaround point described in this hike is the Overlook.

Drive east .3 mile on Sunset Blvd. from Pacific Coast Hwy to Paseo Miramar and turn left (north). Park at the far end of Paseo Miramar Avenue. Parking is limited. Go around the fireroad gate to begin an uphill walk that will gain 850 feet in about a mile. The views to the south are quick to develop as you gain altitude. Santa Monica Bay spreads out below, dotted with hundreds of sails when the wind is up. Farther south, Palos Verdes juts out, and on a clear day Catalina is well in sight. The conglomerate rock on the east of the road was deposited 60 to 70 million years ago during Paleocene times and named the Coal Canyon Formation. The cliff formation in Los Liones Canyon to the left is tilted southeast at an angle of about 75°. The rock area in the canyon is a good lunch spot but requires some scrambling down a short but rocky trail.

The route loses some altitude as it swings around the west side of a hill. It then drops down to a saddle that allows you to stop for the view of Palisades Highlands on the east. The "wirebreak" intersects the fireroad here and is a means of getting to Santa Ynez Canyon below. At one time a power line overhead was the clue to presence of the trail. Two miles from the trailhead, a road branches left and goes 1/2 mile to the Overlook. This high point of land presents an exceptional view of the ocean to the south and of the abrupt manner in which the mountains meet the sea.

Several unmaintained trails start at the Overlook and go through the chaparral that has vigorously regrown since the 1973 Trippet fire. I don't recommend these routes for travel. They are steep, rocky, almost impossible to follow, and covered with dense chaparral. A trail to Los Liones Canyon starts on the east side of the point and follows the ridge southeast, but chaparral hides it well enough to make following it difficult. The ridge southwest is the route of an annual trail-less hike called the "Lemming hike" that is virtually impassable through dense chaparral on steep slopes. This is named after the Lemmings because of their senseless compulsion to get to the ocean. Another steep trail enters upper Los Liones Canyon by a ridge northeast of the Overlook. The beginning of the trail is difficult to find. Normally one would not be inclined to go into this area except to climb on the interesting rock formation below the ridge.

Have lunch at the rocks in the canyon or in the shade of a laurel sumac tree on top of the Overlook before returning the way you came.

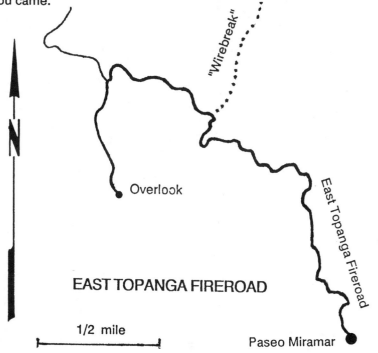

SANTA YNEZ CANYON WATERFALL

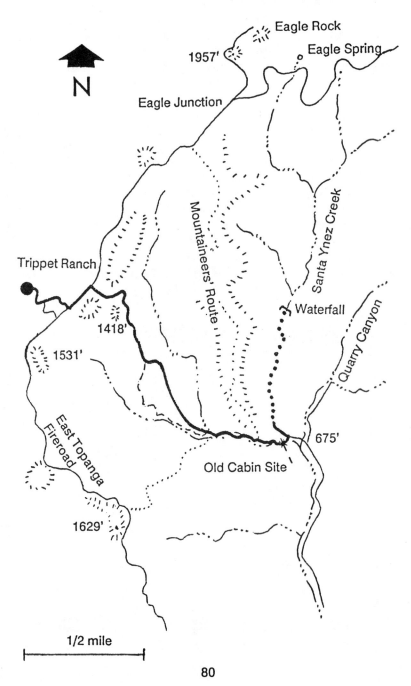

HIKE 7

Distance: 6 miles
Elevation: 1100' gain & loss
Terrain: Fireroad, steep trail, and
              boulder hopping
Time: 3 hours
Trailhead: Trippet Ranch (#1)

Eagle Spring originates in a sandstone glen high on the mountain, and is the source of Santa Ynez Creek. The stream flows all year, and the falls are impressive even when the water is low. The trail in and out of Santa Ynez Canyon is very steep, and the boulders in the canyon below the falls require that you wear good footgear. The route back to Trippet Ranch begins with a long steep climb. Hiking time should be about three hours, not including lunch, for the 6-mile roundtrip.

Follow the trail from the east end of the Ranch parking lot by going uphill in a southerly direction. Turn left at the Latitude and follow the fireroad uphill about 1/4 mile to the Santa Ynez Canyon Trail on the right. Walk down the trail. The fire of November, 1977, burned through this section, transforming a lush stand of chaparral into charred branches. Recovery from the fire began with a wide variety of plant life. Now the chaparral is back.

About 1/3 of the way into the canyon, the footing becomes steep and difficult, so it is necessary to be especially alert to avoid sliding. An alternate trail goes left at this point avoiding the steep section, only to find a steep section later. A couple of trails leave this trail on the ridge and drop down to the stream to the west, there to join the trail headed downstream. Santa Ynez Canyon is in full view to the south. Dense chaparral covers the slopes down to the stream where sycamores and oaks take over. The mouth of the canyon frames the Los Angeles basin and the ocean. The Palisades Highlands housing development nestles in the lower canyon.

The trail makes a left turn upon reaching the bottom of the canyon and follows it downstream. About a half mile beyond, a stream and trail comes in on the left. Turn left and follow the stream 3/4 mile to the base of the waterfall. The trail has been washed out in many places, and the footing may be difficult. The streambed near the falls consists of sandstone ledges and large boulders. Boulders and cliffs below the waterfall partially block the route in two or three places, presenting moderate climbing challenges.

The waterfall pours over a channel in the rock and drops about 15 feet into a pool. Ferns grow on the walls; water-carved cliffs tower above, and a small bit of tree-filtered sky is overhead. A steep and difficult trail leads to the stream above the falls and to more cascades, but the base of the waterfalls is the usual turn-around point.

Hiking down the Santa Ynez Canyon Trail on 14 April 1991.
This group met other groups at Trippet Ranch for the annual "Rendevous." Each group of hikers came on the various trails into the Park, meeting for lunch.

Santa Ynez Waterfall

Trash clean-up crew, 1981, on the Waterfall Trail.
Because waterfalls are delightful places to relax, some visitors forget to pick up after a visit.   Occasionally a group of volunteers get together for a public service day.

Coastal woodfern

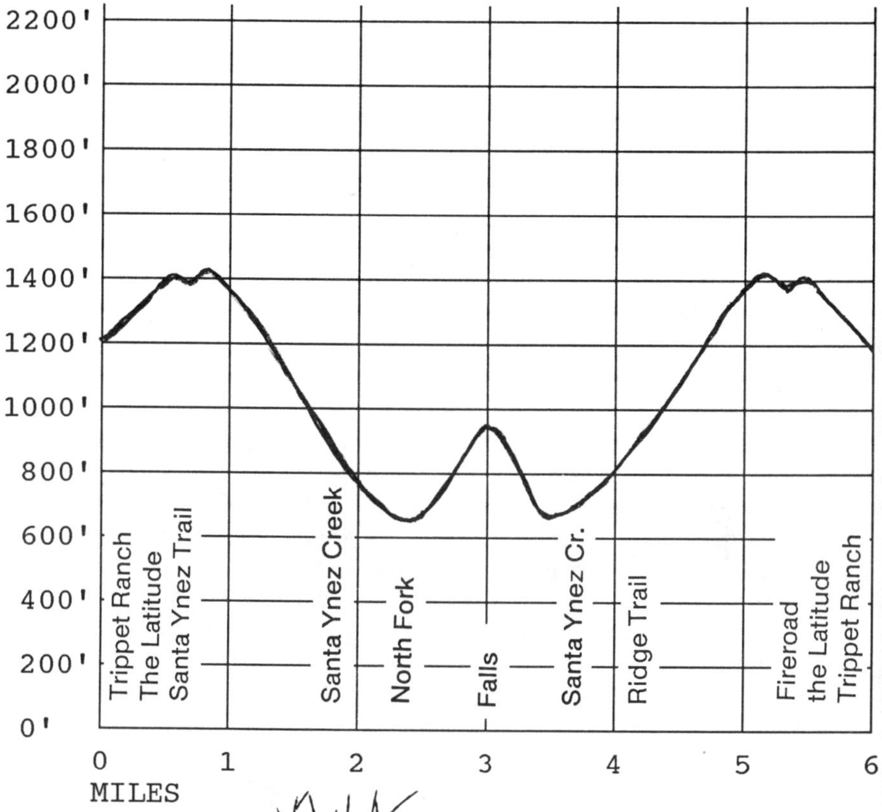
2200'
2000'
1800'
1600'
1400'
1200'
1000'
800'
600'
400'
200'
0'
Trippet Ranch
The Latitude
Santa Ynez Trail
Santa Ynez Creek
North Fork
Falls
Santa Ynez Cr.
Ridge Trail
Fireroad
the Latitude
Trippet Ranch
0
1
2
3
4
5
6
MILES

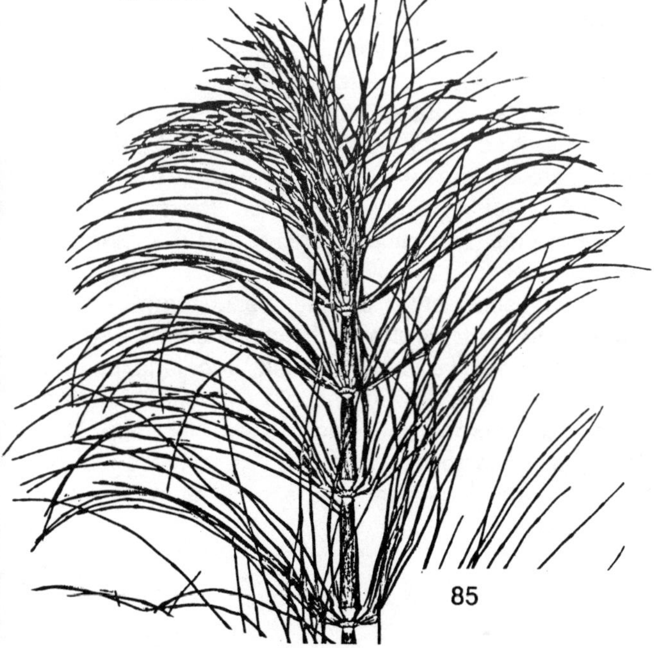

Giant horsetail
Found along the trail below the waterfall

HIKE 8

in Topanga State Park

Maps:	Topanga, topo
Distance:	2½ miles roundtrip
Elevation:	400 feet gain and loss
Terrain:	Trail
Time:	1 hour
Trailhead:	Dead Horse parking lot on Entrada Road (#2)

A short hike—but an interesting hike—the Dead Horse Trail takes us on a tour of the western approach to Trippet Ranch. We will be introduced to dense streamside shade, grasslands, chaparral and oak groves. This particular area was burned in 1925 and 1948. The major fires of recent years have bypassed the area.

The hike begins at the Dead Horse parking lot, 200 yards from Topanga Canyon Boulevard, 1/2 mile north of the Post Office in the town of Topanga. We must take care driving to the parking lot— the turn onto Entrada is sharp and steeply uphill. The turn into the parking lot is on a blind curve. The parking lot is free (1991). The lot closes at night. The trail heads north through chaparral. Except for the imported gravel on the path up from the parking lot, the initial stretch of trail is on solid basalt, a fine grain volcanic rock. Later we will be on sandstone. After 10 minutes on the trail we cross Trippet Creek on a beautiful, rustic, wooden bridge. It was installed in 1986 without so much as disturbing a blade of grass —a highly responsible care for the environment. The streambed is interesting for those who would climb around on rocks and risk some poison oak. Sweet cicely, geranium, grape, and 4 species of fern grow along the banks.

Cross the bridge and soon enter a Chamise chaparral forest. The trail contours along the south and west facing slope of a broad ridge. As the trail heads east we enter an oak woodland on the right and a meadow on the left. Upon reaching a road near the pond, turn right and walk across the earth and rock dam that impounds the water. California roses have become established on the dam. Trippet Ranch is the Park headquarters. A ranger lives in the house south of the parking lot. Restrooms, drinking water, pay phone, picnic area, parking, and Park personnel are available.

We can return the way we came or locate a trail west of the parking lot that crosses a meadow and continues down the south side of the stream. In about 1/4 mile the trail intersects an east-west trail, which if followed north will join the Dead Horse Trail where we turn left and return to our cars.

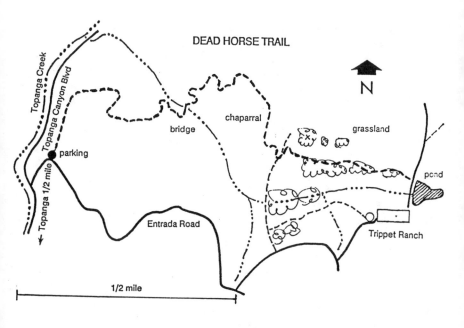

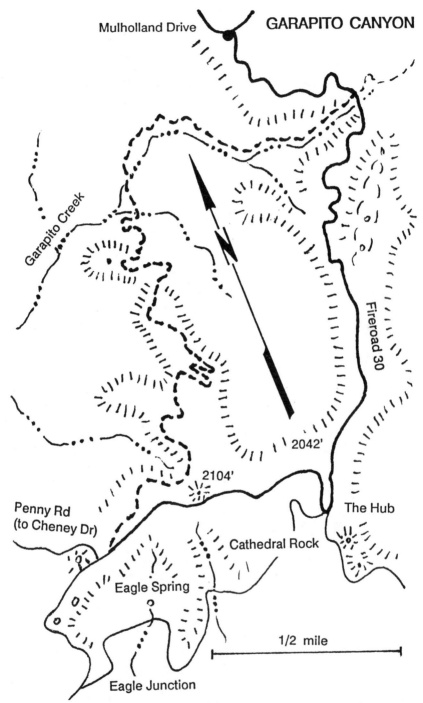

GARAPITO CANYON

Mulholland Drive

Garapito Creek

Fireroad 30

2042'

2104'

Penny Rd
(to Cheney Dr)

The Hub

Cathedral Rock

Eagle Spring

1/2 mile

Eagle Junction

88

HIKE 9

Maps:	Canoga Park, topo
	Topanga, topo
Distance:	6½ miles roundtrip
Elevation:	1200' loss and gain
Time:	3 hours
Trailhead:	Mulholland Drive (#7)

Garapito Canyon is steep, rugged and beautiful. Sierra Club volunteers began building a trail from Fireroad 30 in 1985 and completed it in 1987.

Drive 4 miles east of Topanga Canyon Boulevard on Mulholland Drive into the northern part of Topanga State Park, and park on the right without blocking Fireroad 30. Walk around the fireroad gate and go 1/2 mile to a point where some power lines cross. The trail into upper Garapito Canyon is on the right and begins here. Cross a small meadow then abruptly enter dense chaparral. The entire canyon last burned in 1961 and the chaparral has had time to recover completely. Trail building in 1985 opened sunlit corridors so that dormant seeds that have lain in the duff since the 1961 fire recovery period, could sprout. The spring of 1986 ushered in a riot of giant phacelia, mustard evening primrose, contorted evening primrose, white pincushion, yellow monkey flower, and other fire-following plants along the trail.

In the more than 500 feet of elevation loss, the trail takes us through a lot of chaparral and occasional patches of coastal sage scrub. Whenever we are near the streambed we will see sycamores, and at one place several cottonwoods. Geologically, the streambed and ravines are the Coal Canyon Formation, a marine sequence of sandstone, siltstone, and pebbly conglomerate. This formed during late Paleocene and Eocene times, 60-50 million years ago. The trail follows side stream channels at times, allowing us the opportunity of getting our feet wet during and after storms. The trail crosses the main streambed, goes up and around a shoulder, and back down to a stretch along the stream to an oak grove. At this point we have walked about 1-3/4 miles from the trailhead—take a rest—we are

Rugged Garapito Canyon drains into Topanga Canyon. The Garapito Trail begins at the top of the canyon, drops down to the bottom, then climbs out to a point near Eagle Rock.

about to start uphill, gaining 700 feet in the next mile and a half. A massive buttress, or ridge, drops down from Peak 2104 to our present location in the canyon. The trail works its way up the ridge at a comfortable walking grade, making switchbacks as it goes. Along one section of the lower trail we look across an arroyo at a spectacular conglomerate cliff. Later, after a couple of switchbacks, we find ourselves above and near the edge of the cliff. This hike offers many excuses to stop and rest. The panorama below unrolls continuously as we climb through the most dense mature chaparral in the area. (I was going to say "in the world" but that may not be true.) We continue upward and get an idea that the crest is near when we go through some open spaces of California buckwheat.

Upon reaching Eagle Spring Loop road, turn left. We might elect to go on a short side trip to the top of Eagle Rock from this point. If so we turn right, walk slightly uphill 650 feet, then walk over a rise on the east and climb the backside of Eagle Rock. The view of Santa Ynez Canyon, to the south, and the ocean is dramatic. The fireroad toward Trippet Ranch and East Topanga Fireroad are visible and so is more of the southern half of the Park. Look for silver lotus plants in bloom from March through June, growing in cracks in the sandstone of Eagle Rock.

The route out is east to the "Hub," about 1 mile from where Penny Road intersects Eagle Spring Loop road. Enroute we pass the highest point on today's hike near Peak 2104. Look at the road near the peak. The pattern of the rock is the result of the slow cooling of molten lava as it intruded through cracks into the sandstone about 15 million years ago. This lava is diabase. We've given it the common name "Onion Rock" because it exfoliates concentrically somewhat like an onion would. At the Hub, turn left and walk 2 miles to Mulholland Drive and our cars.

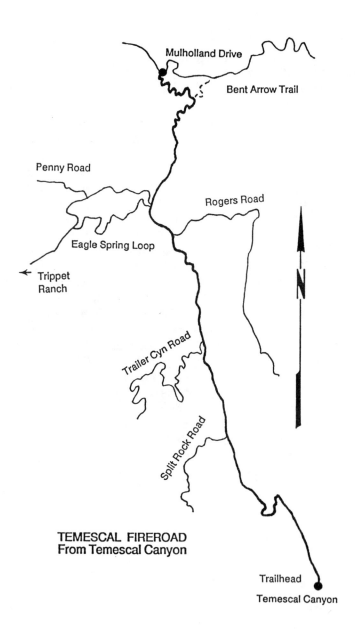

Mulholland Drive

Bent Arrow Trail

Penny Road

Rogers Road

Eagle Spring Loop

← Trippet
Ranch

N

Trailer Cyn Road

Split Rock Road

TEMESCAL FIREROAD
From Temescal Canyon

Trailhead
Temescal Canyon

HIKE 10

Distance:	17.5 mi. roundtrip
Elevation:	2300 ft. gain and loss
Terrain:	Fireroad
Time:	8 hours including lunch
Trailhead:	Temescal Canyon (#16)

This hike starts at the Pacific Palisades Conference Center on Temescal Road and goes to Mulholland Drive and back by way of Fireroad 30. The Conference Center and some of the ridge are private property, so the use of this trail is subject to conditions determined by the owners. As of this writing, conditions that are suitable in the Park are acceptable in the private area. Watch for any posted notices and comply with them. Because you go and return by the same route, you have the option of turning around short of the destination. Or you could arrange a car shuttle at the north end. The hike crosses the Park in a south to north direction by use of a dominant ridge. You will see excellent views of Santa Ynez, Temescal, Rustic, and Garapito Canyons. The San Fernando Valley can be seen from the north end of the hike and the Los Angeles Basin from the south. This route clearly shows the expanse of wildland that exists within the city.

Sign-in on the roster at the entrance to the Center and walk to the left of the road on a trail that passes one house then goes uphill. A fork in the trail gives you an option of two routes. The west option features a "View Point," the east option features a "waterfall." Either way is suitable — they meet up on the ridge. You might elect to go one way and come back the other. Assume that you take the right fork and stay in the canyon, you will contour north along a steep slope overlooking the Conference Center houses below. Beyond the houses the trail angles back down to the stream. The route follows a washed out road as it continues up Temescal Creek, then climbs through the narrow gorge of the canyon. The gorge offers some interesting features. A thin waterfall on the east side of the trail could become serious after a rainstorm. Cliff forming conglomerate rock adds a rugged accent to the steep canyon walls, and Temescal Creek cascades down a narrow gorge.

The trail crosses the stream where a wooden bridge once spanned the 15 to 20 foot distance from bank to bank. The Mandeville fire of 1978 came through Temescal Canyon and burned the bridge, so now you must use your own resources to get to the other side. The trail crosses the stream, makes a switchback to the left as it goes steeply up the wall of the canyon, then tops out on a ridge going northwest. The fireroad stays near the crest of the ridge, gaining altitude moderately. Upper Temescal Canyon to the east is totally undeveloped whereas both Pulga Canyon and Santa Ynez Canyon to the west show building activity. This part of the hike was in the path of the 1978 Mandeville fire and was completely blackened. The recovery by resprouting chaparral and flowering plants is striking, and few signs of the fire are evident. Pass Skull Rock and take time for a closer look. You might exercise your imagination some, but from the right viewpoint this rock looks like a skull. Continue north on the trail.

Split Rock Road comes in on the left, and about 1 mile farther north, Trailer Canyon Road comes up from Santa Ynez Canyon. A microwave facility, locally called "Radio Peak," is about half way

between the two points. The route continues north on a reasonably level grade, intersecting with Rogers Road about 1½ miles beyond the Trailer Canyon intersection. The highest point in the Park, Temescal Peak (2126'), is near the intersection. The peak may be climbed by a short but steep firebreak for a good view of Temescal, Rustic and Santa Ynez Canyons.

Continue north on the fireroad, which is a segment of the Backbone Trail at this point passing Cathedral Rock in 1/2 mile, then on to Hub Junction—a four way intersection. The left road goes to Trippet Ranch by way of Eagle Spring; the next left road goes to Trippet Ranch by way of Eagle Rock, and the road straight ahead is a continuation of Fireroad 30, the route of this hike. One-and-a-half miles from the Hub, the Bent Arrow Trail has its beginning by clinging to the wall of upper Rustic Canyon and working its way east, eventually to parallel Mulholland Drive. Stay on Fireroad 30 reaching Mulholland Drive at entrance designated #7.

You have just walked through a wilderness area—all within Los Angeles city limits—and probably have met other hikers and some animals but not many distractions. You have earned the beauties of the recesses of the Park by hard physical work and must feel a sense of accomplishment that few others do. You should be tired. Return the way you came.

"Looking into Rustic Canyon from Cathedral Rock"

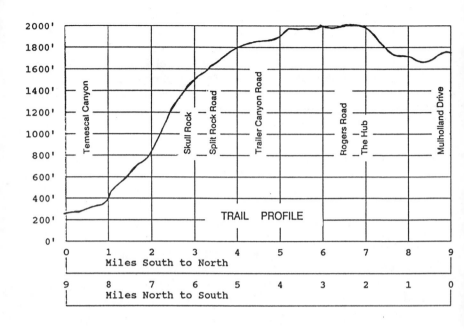

TRAIL PROFILE

2000'
1800'
1600'
1400'
1200'
1000'
800'
600'
400'
200'
0'

Temescal Canyon
Skull Rock
Split Rock Road
Trailer Canyon Road
Rogers Road
The Hub
Mulholland Drive

0 1 2 3 4 5 6 7 8 9
Miles South to North

9 8 7 6 5 4 3 2 1 0
Miles North to South

A scrub oak (Quercus dumosa) in September as the acorns are ripe

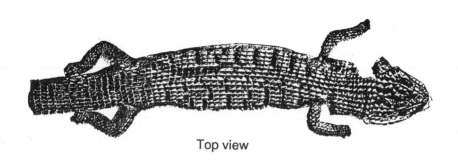

Top view

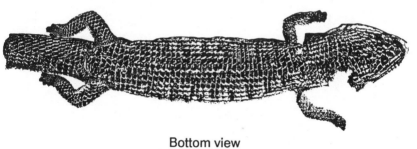

Bottom view

Once in a while you may find where a lizard crawled out and left its skin. The dark shadow in the upper view is the tail turned partially inside out, and left in the dried skin case.

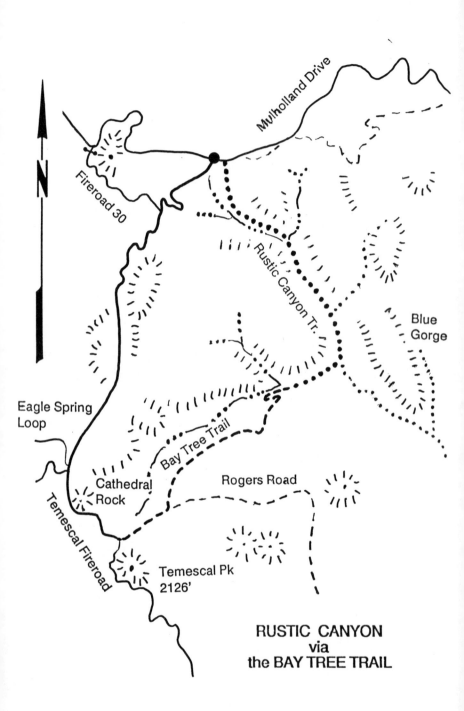

N

Mulholland Drive

Fireroad 30

Rustic Canyon Tr.

Blue Gorge

Eagle Spring Loop

Bay Tree Trail

Rogers Road

Temescal Fireroad

Cathedral Rock

Temescal Pk 2126'

RUSTIC CANYON
via
the BAY TREE TRAIL

HIKE 11

via the Bay Tree Trail
from Mulholland Drive

Distance:	6 miles roundtrip
Elevation:	1200' gain and loss
Terrain:	Trail, fireroad, and streambed
Time:	2-3/4 hours
Trailhead:	Mulholland Drive (#8)

This hike down into Rustic Canyon requires trail finding abilities. The route in the canyon is not marked, and because of winter rains the trail is not well defined. It is best to go on this hike with an experienced leader and learn the route before taking the trip alone. Most of the hike is in the Park, but Rustic Canyon belongs to the Sanitation Dept. Current use of the canyon is on the same basis as the Park.

The hike begins on the Bent Arrow Trail at Mulholland Drive, 4.8 miles east of Topanga Canyon Blvd., and contours southwest along a steep slope. Walking along the Bent Arrow Trail gives us an early opportunity to note the rugged Rustic Canyon below. Our last leg of the hike will come up the canyon.

At the end of Bent Arrow Trail we reach Fireroad 30, turn left and walk on a somewhat level dirt road for the next half hour. Before reaching Hub Junction we come to an uphill grade that gains 300 feet. Garapito Canyon is on the right, Rustic on the left. We stay on Fireroad 30 and continue south at Hub Junction. The road is also known as Temescal fireroad. The two roads leading west make up the Eagle Spring Loop; the lower road passes the spring, the upper road goes by Eagle Rock.

As we go south on Temescal fireroad, Cathedral Rock is on the left. A trail up the slope on the south side leads to a protected area in the rocks. This is a good lunch spot, but we will not have walked far enough on this hike to have earned a lunch break, so we continue. Ten minutes beyond Cathedral Rock we watch for Rogers Road on our left. Various signs tell us it is:

4.4 miles to Temescal Conference Grounds (Trailhead #16)
2.4 miles to Mulholland Drive (Trailhead #7)

Bay Tree Trail goes through a canopy of Bay trees. The aroma as you walk on the leaves will stay in your memory.

4 miles to the Ranger Station (Trailhead #1)
1.8 miles to Eagle Junction, and
6 miles to Will Rogers State Historic Park (Trailhead #15).
We turn left and walk downhill on Rogers Road about 400 yards.

When the road levels out we look for the Bay Tree Trail on the left. The trail drops down through heavy chaparral toward the stream, losing about 800 feet in one mile. The variety of vegetation is quite noticeable; chaparral dominates the slopes, and riparian woodlands shelter the streams coming down the mountain. Flowers cover the open spaces and are along the trail in spring. The lower part of the trail enters a Bay tree forest that continues down to the West fork of Rustic, and a good lunch spot.

The trail makes a couple of switchbacks at the bottom, then reaches the streambed. From this point on a trail may or may not be evident, depending upon what the previous winter rains and flooding have done. We time ourselves going downstream from the base of the Bay Tree Trail. After 10 minutes we look for the main fork of Rustic Creek, coming down from the north. At this point we turn left and go up the main fork. The confluence of the two streams is obvious to me but we must stay alert. Willows in the streambed, and poison oak along the banks have distracted some hikers and they have missed the turn. (If you were to do this hike in the reverse direction, the entrance into West Fork is obscured.) At this point you might care to take a one hour side trip and go to Blue Gorge. If so, go downstream on a gentle grade. After fifteen minutes look closely for a canyon on your left. Follow this canyon upstream on a sometimes trail. The canyon narrows and you will climb over some rocks as you reach a couple of small waterfalls. A five-foot waterfall calls for rock climbing ability to continue. At the top of the falls you are in Blue Gorge. Look for Maple trees growing from the rocks on both sides of the gorge. Humboldt lilies abound.

Return to the spot where you entered the main canyon and continue upstream in Rustic Canyon.

For the most part, the streambed is broad, flat, and gravelly. Many rocks and some downed trees cause us to take care in walking. The sides of the canyon are of Santa Monica Slate, laid down as deep sea deposits about 150 million years ago. Some of the rocks and boulders are granite and quartzite that have been washed down from the head of the canyon. Coast live oaks and sycamore trees shade the canyons. A few black cottonwoods grow in the west fork. Willows and mulefat grow in the gravel of the streambed. The stream banks are home to a wide variety of flowers. Ferns grow well on shady slopes and the cliffs, and chaparral covers all the steep slopes away from the canyon.

Twenty-five to thirty minutes after starting up the main fork, we look for an indistinct trail on the right. There, a small side canyon comes down from Mulholland Drive. We follow the side canyon about 200 feet and the trail becomes well defined, then goes steeply up a ridge to Mulholland. The car should be in sight a few hundred yards on the left.

Down in the canyon we have had several chances to take the wrong route. One trail leaves the streambed and goes to a firebreak on the ridge south of Gizmo Peak. In the event you take this trail you can follow it to Mulholland. Another common wrong turn can occur at a side canyon about 1/3 mile downstream of the correct route. A faint trail in this canyon disappears and the brush becomes dense enough to discourage any hiker.

"Rustic" is a mild definition of this wild and rugged area. I am amazed that such an isolated and remote canyon exists within the city limits of Los Angeles. Hikers have become lost in the canyon so even with these instructions as a guide, my recommendation is to take your first hike into the canyon with someone who knows the way.

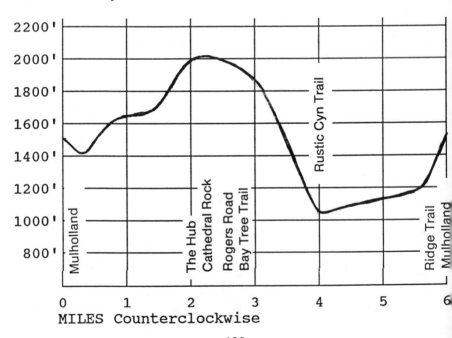

One of the small waterfalls in Blue Gorge

EAGLE SPRING LOOP
via Fireroad 30

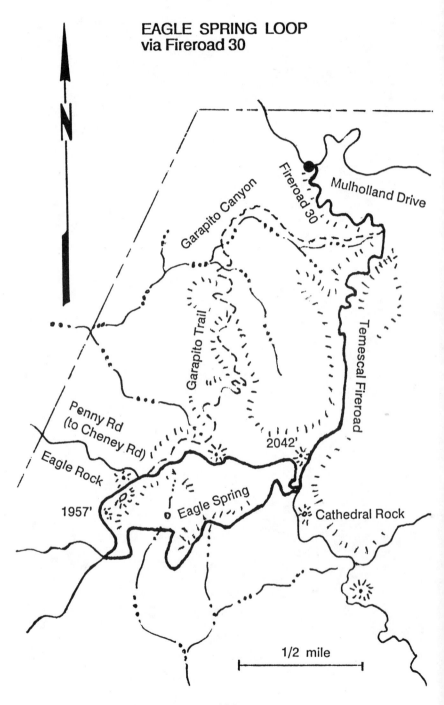

N

Garapito Canyon

Fireroad 30

Mulholland Drive

Garapito Trail

Temescal Fireroad

Penny Rd
(to Cheney Rd)

Eagle Rock

1957'

2042'

Eagle Spring

Cathedral Rock

1/2 mile

HIKE 12

Distance:	7 miles roundtrip
Elevation:	1000' gain and loss
Terrain:	Fireroad
Time:	2-3/4 hours
Trailhead:	Mulholland Drive (#7)

This is a trip in Topanga State Park that is on a fireroad all the way and although steep in a few places is a good introductory hike.

Drive to the beginning of Fireroad 30 on dirt Mulholland Drive. This point is 4.0 miles east from Topanga Canyon Blvd. and 6.4 miles west of the overpass at the San Diego Freeway.

Walk around the fireroad gate south onto Fireroad 30 and go two miles until coming to "Hub Junction," an intersection of four roads. Of the three choices available take the one on the immediate right and go uphill. You will soon be on an east-west ridge that separates Garapito Canyon on the north from Santa Ynez Canyon on the south. On a reasonably clear day you may see Santa Monica Bay and the coast line all the way to Palos Verdes Peninsula. If you have a compass and can use it for sighting, Santa Catalina Island is 180° true (165° magnetic) from the ridge. On the clearest day of the year you might see the small Santa Barbara Island and San Nicolas Island farther out.

Continue west along the ridge. Penny Road comes in on the right and is another way of entering Topanga State Park. Just beyond this road but on the left is Eagle Rock, overlooking upper Santa Ynez Canyon. A short side trip will take you to the top of the rock, its sculptured caves, and the impressive view of the valley below.

Continue along the fireroad going downhill. Notice a rock formation on your left a few hundred yards after leaving Eagle Rock. "Onion Rock," because it exfoliates in concentric layers, is a part of a volcanic intrusion. Diabase intrusions are also found on East Topanga Fireroad. Upon reaching Eagle Junction, turn left and continue downhill toward Eagle Spring. Eagle Rock looms high overhead, dominating upper Santa Ynez Canyon with its imposing mass and exposed cliffs. Eagle Spring is identified by a large wooden water storage tank. The spring itself is upstream a short distance by trail. A pipeline comes down from the spring to the wooden tank. Enough water leaks out to keep the ground wet. Beautiful patches of Poison Oak thrive in the area.

Continue along the fireroad as it contours through the chaparral toward Hub Junction. The moderate elevation gain is 400 feet in a little more than a mile. As you near Hub Junction you can see a lofty crag on the ridge to the right. "Cathedral Rock" holds a sheltered recess within its protective walls that makes an excellent lunch stop. This is south on the Temescal Fireroad and not on the loop of this hike, but does make an interesting short side trip.

Eagle Rock

At The Hub go north on Fireroad 30, retracing your steps for the two miles back to the roadhead. The walk is pleasant along this ridge road with the isolation of Rustic Canyon to the east and Garapito Canyon to the west.

Cathedral Rock taken from Fireroad 30 north of the Hub

HIKE 13

CABALLERO CANYON
Ridge Trail Loop

Distance:	4½ miles roundtrip
Elevation:	1000' gain and loss
Terrain:	Steep trail, Fireroad
Time:	2 hours
Trailhead:	Reseda Blvd. (#11)

A steep trail on a Chaparral ridge is the main feature of this short but strenuous hike.

We start by driving to the south end of Reseda Boulevard in Tarzana, and parking.

About 200 yards north of where the golf course road enters Reseda Boulevard look for an entrance gate on the east side of the street. Subdivision construction activity will last a few more years so expect some changes in trailhead location. Look for a sign that shows the trail's beginning. Walk in and turn right staying on the trail that parallels Reseda Boulevard. Opposite the spot where the golf course road enters Reseda look left for a trail that goes straight up a ridge. This is an uphill grind so my head will be down and my vision will concentrate on the rocks underfoot and the plants at the trail's edge. This unmaintained trail isn't for everyone.

Most of the lower ridge is geologically Modelo shale overlaying Tuna Canyon Formation. The dividing line between the two formations is not distinct so we are likely to notice the formations alternately. About half way to Mulholland Drive we begin to walk on Santa Monica Slate. In at least one point we cross over some more Modelo shale. After a gain of 880 feet we drop down from a little peak and go through a Toyon tunnel, then uphill for a minute to Mulholland Drive.

At Mulholland turn right and walk one mile to Fireroad 28, gradually losing 300' of altitude. Turn right onto Fireroad 28 and follow it down into Caballero Canyon.

Caballero Canyon with its trails is an important entry to the northern part of Topanga State Park. The trails into Rustic Canyon, Sullivan Canyon and Ridge, Fireroad 30 and its offshoot trails, can be reached from the dirt section of Mulholland Drive. Dirt Mulholland Drive is not always passable for vehicular traffic, leaving the trail system out of Caballero Canyon the route of choice.

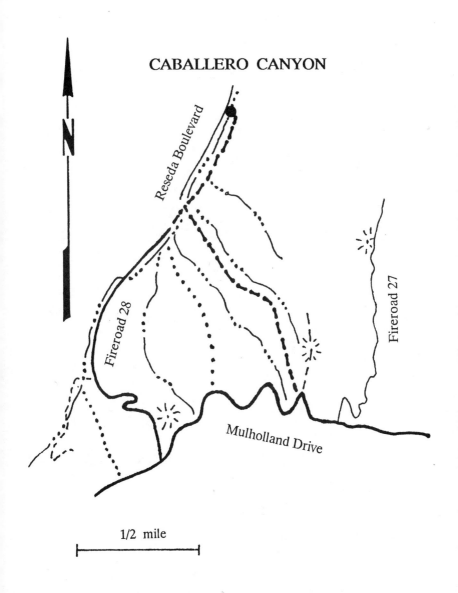

CABALLERO CANYON

1/2 mile

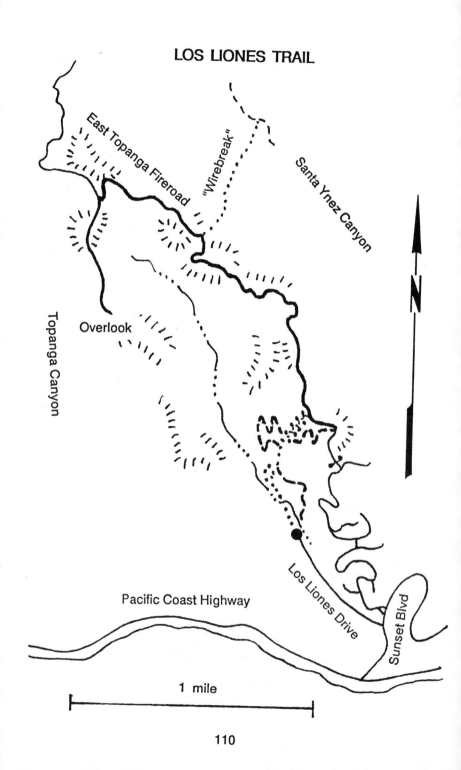

LOS LIONES TRAIL

East Topanga Fireroad

"Wirebreak"

Santa Ynez Canyon

N

Topanga Canyon

Overlook

Los Liones Drive

Sunset Blvd

Pacific Coast Highway

1 mile

HIKE 14

Distance:	6 miles roundtrip
Elevation:	1500' gain and loss
Terrain:	Trail and fireroad
Time:	3 hours
Trailhead:	Los Liones Drive (#22)

Los Liones Canyon is a rugged, steep sloped, secluded area near civilization yet apart from the urban scene. A hiking trail in this part of Topanga State Park is welcome.

Drive east .3 mile on Sunset Blvd. from the Pacific Coast Highway to Los Liones Drive and turn left. Park at the end of the street in a small parking area, avoiding the Church parking lot. Go around the fence to the left by the lemonade berry bush and follow the trail north along the intermittent stream. The trail existing in April 1991 is in the process of being re-routed. I'll quote present instructions, then new instructions for later in the year and after. The Sierra Club Task Force trail crew is consistent and does good work so look for a new trail soon. Here's the old trail: " About 300 yards from the trailhead we make an abrupt turn right and go up steeply. The trail makes many switchbacks through chaparral and temporarily levels out on a mesa after gaining 300 feet. After this brief respite we go into a bigpod ceanothus forest and gain another 400 feet as the trail makes countless switchbacks up the steep hillside. Abruptly, the East Topanga Fireroad nears and we turn left and follow it uphill. The road continues uphill until easing up in about two-thirds of a mile and a 500 foot gain. About 20 minutes later we look for a trail that follows the top of a ridge heading south. One half mile along the ridge brings us to the 'Overlook,' an area with a great view of the ocean and the seacoast. Palos Verdes Penninsula and Catalina Island are visible on clear days."

Here's the new trail: "Within 100 feet of the fence turn right and cross the canyon. The trail angles left as it starts a gentle climb along the west-facing slope of the ridge. Ten minutes later the new trail temporarily merges with the old trail. After a few hundred feet it leaves the old trail to continue north. Gaining

111

Santa Monica Bay from the Los Liones Trail

Resting at the Overlook

altitude at a moderate rate, the trail makes a few switchbacks as it heads north on the west-facing slope."

The 1973 Trippet fire burned the slope south of the Overlook. For a few years a passable route went down the south ridge, but the chaparral has recovered so that the route is not in use.

Return the way we came but take the time to look west into Topanga Canyon and the 1300 foot drop to the stream. One-half mile along East Topanga Fireroad we can look left down the "Wirebreak" and see Santa Ynez Canyon.

This hike has some steep sections of trail that give most of us a good workout — but I have seen people run it.

Big pod ceanothus dominates the upper slopes in Los Liones Canyon

SANTA YNEZ CANYON
EAST TOPANGA FIREROAD
via the "Wirebreak"

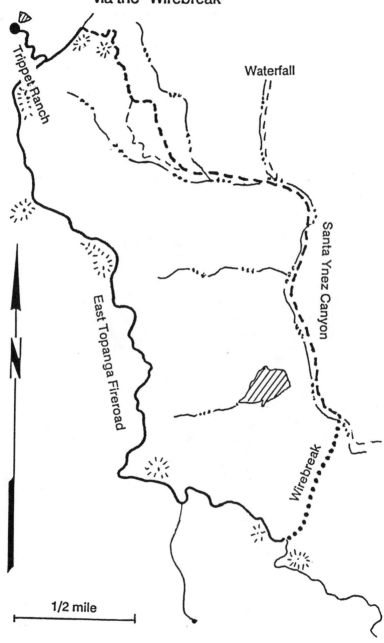

Trippet Ranch

Waterfall

Santa Ynez Canyon

East Topanga Fireroad

Wirebreak

N

1/2 mile

HIKE 15

Distance:	8 miles roundtrip
Elevation:	1700' gain and loss
Terrain:	Trail, firebreak and fireroad
Time:	3¼ hours
Trailhead:	Trippet Ranch (#1)

The "Wirebreak" is an unrelenting, steep grind and should be taken seriously. Loose footing requires care either uphill or downhill on this slope. For me, hiking boots are a "must" on this hike.

On Highway 27 just north of the town of Topanga turn east on Entrada Road. Once on Entrada Road turn left at every street intersection. It is 1.1 miles to the entrance of Topanga State Park. This is where you will park your car.

The hiking trail goes uphill from the east end of the parking lot. Turn left upon reaching the "Latitude," a point on the fireroad along the saddle. This road leads gently uphill through a grove of coast live oaks. About 300-400 yards after leaving the Latitude there is another saddle that allows a good view of Santa Ynez Canyon on the right. Take the trail that crosses over to a little ridge then, after a left turn, drops down into Santa Ynez Canyon. The upper part goes through part of the area burned in the fire of November 1977 and for a few years will be covered with wild flowers every spring until the chaparral returns. Starting down the trail presents a continuing change in the panorama of the lower canyon. Dense stands of chamise, ceanothus, sumac and toyon can be seen on the slopes to the west; massive sandstone can be seen on ridges below; and on a clear day the ocean is framed by the mouth of the canyon.

After dropping 700' rather steeply, the trail enters a cool riparian woodland shaded with oaks and sycamores. The trail makes a sharp turn left and becomes almost level as it gently follows the stream. Blackberry vines, humboldt Lilies, and a myriad other plants

The "Wirebreak"

carpet the banks of the stream. Farther on down, just before the stream we are following joins with the Santa Ynez north fork, an old cabin site is off to the left in amongst some poison oak. About all that is visible now are two rock chimneys, one with a fireplace.

Continue downstream for a good 3/4 mile more and come to a large culvert which you walk through. At times the water level prevents using the culvert, and even at best, the growth of vegetation downstream of the culvert makes walking difficult. Many hikers prefer to cross the road and locate a trail leading down the bank to the streambed level. This is in the area of a housing development but if you stay down along the stream, none of the sense of the primitive is lost. Come out of culvert on the left side of the stream and continue for about 1/4 mile, at which time look very closely for the trail on the other side of the stream that leads up to the firebreak.

The "wirebreak," so called because of the power line that once was nearby, is 800 feet of elevation gain in less than 1/2 mile — just continuous uphill misery. Once on top, however, the road that you find is level by comparison. Turn right and follow this East Topanga Fireroad for about 3 miles to a junction where the road drops down to Trippet Ranch.

This section affords a view overlooking both Topanga Canyon on the west and Santa Ynez Canyon on the east as well as an ocean view to the south.

The variety on this hike is emphatic: oak woodland, chaparral, and riparian woodland; pristine wilderness bordered by a housing development; canyon depths and lofty ridge viewpoints; strenuous exertion and relaxed enjoyment — a full range of experience.

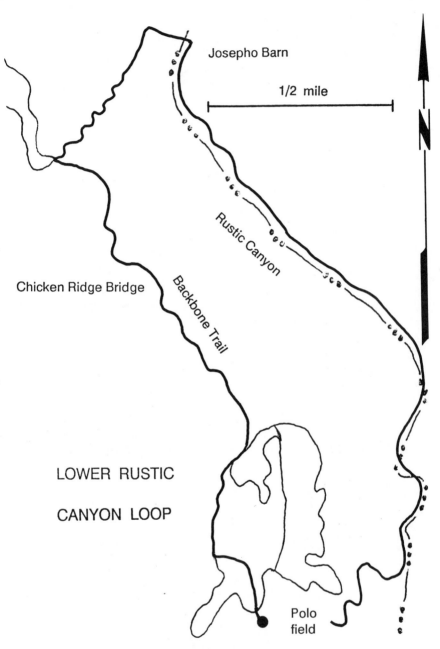

Josepho Barn

1/2 mile

N

Rustic Canyon

Chicken Ridge Bridge

Backbone Trail

LOWER RUSTIC

CANYON LOOP

Polo field

Will Rogers State Historic Park

118

HIKE 16

LOWER RUSTIC CANYON LOOP
from Will Rogers State Historic Park

Distance:	5 miles
Elevation:	1050' gain and loss
Terrain:	Steep trails, fireroad, boulder hopping
Time:	2 hours, 45 minutes
Trailhead:	Will Rogers State Historic Park (#15)

This hike quickly takes you to Rogers Ridge then down to the bottom of Rustic Canyon. The steep trails and some boulder hopping in the canyon will challenge your stamina. You will find class 2 rock climbing in the lower canyon and some wet stream crossing when the water is running. If heights bother you, Rogers Ridge will make you nervous.

Begin your hike at Will Rogers State Historic Park. If coming by RTD bus, get off at the Evans Road stop on Sunset Boulevard and walk up the trail to the polo field. This will add about 1/2 mile each way. If you drive, park in the lot. Start near the tennis courts west of Park Headquarters and head uphill on a trail bordered with a white wooden fence. Upon reaching the fireroad, you are given a choice of turning left and walking on a gentle route, or crossing the road onto a steep rough trail. Take the steeper route — you need the mental preparation for some steeper trails ahead. The trail heads north by west, short-cutting the fireroad. Turn right when you next reach the fireroad higher on the ridge. At the next fork in the road go straight ahead (left of the two options). In a few minutes another fork to the left gives a glimpse of a Kiosk with information on the Backbone Trail. Go to the Kiosk and start uphill to the north. If at anytime you take a wrong turn up to this point, you are likely to end up on Inspiration Point. Look north and see the Kiosk and the trail.

The trail up Rogers Ridge is gravelly, steep and rutted. Views south become spectacular and only get better as you gain altitude. After one and a half miles you cross Chicken Ridge bridge. Much of the excitement of this ridge is gone now that the bridge increases the safety. Will Rogers and Anatol Josepho are reported to have designed this route, but had also scouted out a lower trail to the east to avoid the knife-edge of Chicken Ridge. The Chicken Ridge route became the riding trail between the two ranches — the trail you are on today. Beyond the bridge the trail hangs on a steep rock slope. Severe trail erosion makes the footing difficult so we take care. In less than one-half mile you walk along a scrub oak ridge and come to a trail junction. The Backbone Trail splits going north with one route on the ridge; the other contouring on the slope facing Rivas Canyon. You turn right and walk down to Rustic Canyon. The trail is steep, losing almost 700' in less than a mile. One needs to recognize poison oak on this trail and in lower Rustic Canyon. Some great views of Rustic Canyon develop as you descend. Sycamore, cottonwood and walnut trees show a ribbon of green along Rustic Creek every spring. The trail crosses the stream and heads toward a large wooden barn enclosed by a cyclone fence. A large, attractive, multi-trunked sycamore shades the upstream side of the barn. Look for some coast redwoods planted here years ago. The other buildings of the Josepho ranch burned in a fire.

Josepho Barn in Rustic Canyon

The trail downstream drops into the streambed at times, but for the most part stays on the left bank. Ruins of burned-out homes and old foundations are spaced along the bank. The large two-story metal framed structure was part of the Murphy complex. It appears to have been a workshop on the ground floor, and dormitory above. The concrete building to the south housed a power station with two large generators. A large steel diesel fuel tank still stands hidden in the trees of a side canyon. A series of concrete steps will take you up the slope, all the way to Sullivan Ridge west if you can find the route.

Farther south, a burned cabin is all that remains of Will Rogers' hideaway. The double fireplace remains among the rubble. No one lives in this part of the canyon now. Look for some large bay trees. You'll pass by some large jointed cactus, and be somewhat careful as you pass a beehive in a bay tree.

The trail forks right and crosses the stream. The left fork goes to the top of the dam built by the Santa Monica Land and Water Company about 1900. The dam is now silted to the top so no water is impounded. Go around the dam by trail. You can go back up the stream to the base of the dam for a look.

The route downstream more or less follows the creek but can no longer be called a trail. You will get your feet wet when the canyon narrows, and will resort to class 2 rock climbing on occasion. Will Rogers built a road up the creek among these rocks. A narrow and steep detour around the dam allowed him to drive through Rustic Canyon in his Ford touring car. He built a small log cabin in the canyon. Floods have removed the road and fire has

taken the log cabin. You will wonder how anyone would have the optimism to put a road through this narrow, rocky gorge. About the time you have had enough of wet boots and slipping on rocks, a trail takes you uphill about 1/3 mile to the east end of the polo field. Many people walk to the stream and back on this, the Rustic Canyon Trail, to Rustic Canyon. Secluded ravines, wood bridges, cliffs, rocks, and the canyon with a stream makes this a special place.

Chimney of Roger's Retreat
in Rustic Canyon

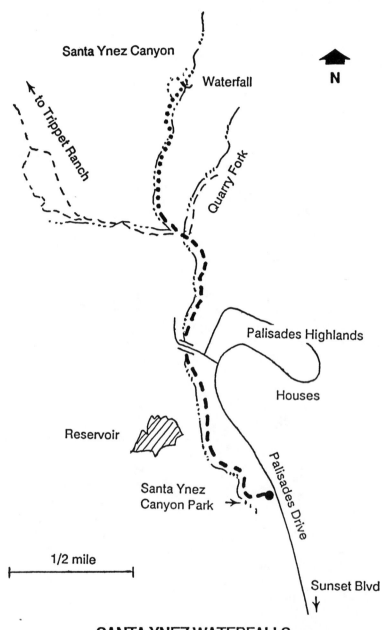

SANTA YNEZ WATERFALLS
from Santa Ynez Canyon Park

HIKE 17

Distance:	4 miles roundtrip
Elevation:	300' gain and loss
Terrain:	Trail and Boulder hopping
Time:	2½ hours
Trailhead:	Palisades Drive (#18)

This is not a strenuous trip at all unless you elect to climb up the waterfalls in the canyon. The footing can be difficult because the winter rains wipe out trails and bring down small trees and brush.

The trailhead is reached from Sunset Blvd. Turn north on Palisades Drive (.3 mile from Pacific Coast Highway), and in 1-3/4 miles a sign on the left indicates entry to Santa Ynez State Park. Park outside and walk in, reaching the stream in a minute or two.

Walk upstream, initially staying on a trail that follows along the east bank. Later on, the trail crosses and recrosses the stream many times, and even loses its identity as a trail on occasion. When in doubt, use the stream as a guide. One-half mile from the trailhead you walk through a cement culvert, then past a cement apron water drainage on the right and continue the gentle upstream walk. In the last few years vegetation has taken over the trail below the culvert, making it difficult to travel for most of us and impossible for others. A makeshift trail has developed up the east bank so you can cross the road above the culvert and down a trail to the stream. If the route below the culvert doesn't suit you, get into your car and go uphill on Palisades Drive to Vereda de la Montura. Turn left and park near the Park entrance. This is trailhead #19.

The canyon narrows, and some cliff forming sandstone rock becomes prominent on both sides of the stream. Caves, or rockshelters, can be seen near stream level as well as higher on the cliffs. An intermittent stream comes down steeply from the right. At that point, and for 100 feet, are found limestone outcroppings along the trail and showing in the stream.

Santa Ynez Canyon Trail upstream of the culvert.

Santa Ynez Waterfall

Continue upstream and you soon come to a gate. Immediately beyond the gate is a fork in the stream and the trail. Take the left fork as the right fork goes to Quarry Canyon. Before crossing the stream notice a large sandstone rock that has a mortar hole on the top side. The size and shape indicate that this was used by the Indians for grinding acorns. Cross the stream and continue 100 yards, reaching another fork in the trail. This time, turn right, cross the stream, and follow the north fork upstream. An old Cabin Site is on the point of land between the streams above their junction. Two stone chimneys about 30 feet apart are all that remain of the buildings. Trees have grown up into what was once the building and have all but completely hidden the chimneys. The vegetation is so thick that there is some difficulty getting to the area. Part of the vegetation is poison oak; and to further dissuade careless exploration, look for a resident rattler on the indistinct trail leading to the site.

Twenty minutes on the north fork of boulder hopping and some trail, takes you through a lot of poison oak, ferns, humboldt lilies and water-loving plants. Look for Pacific tree-frogs on overcast, cool days, or in sheltered places; tadpoles can be found in April and May.

Rock Shelter in Lower Santa Ynez Canyon

When hearing the "kreck-eck" of the Pacific tree-frog you might expect to see a large animal, if measured by the sound volume; but look for a 1½ inch long frog that blends with the surroundings and is not likely to be close to a tree. Also notice the characteristic black stripe that runs from the nostril to behind the eye.

The canyon walls become steep and rugged, the stream narrows, and you feel that the waterfalls are close. Several small falls come first, and you are challenged in climbing up some rock; then around to the right of a turn in the canyon is a beautiful, twelve foot waterfall. Occasionally climbers with ropes will continue farther and even go to the source of the stream at Eagle Spring; but this is the turnaround point of this hike because of the difficult rock climbing.

Return the way you came, and remind yourself to come back again at the tail end of a good rainstorm for a real spectacle.

HIKE 18

Distance:	1 mile roundtrip
Elevation:	100' gain and loss
Terrain:	Fireroad
Time:	30 minutes
Trailhead:	Mulholland Drive (#10)

On Mulholland Drive go to a large parking area on the south side, across from Fireroad 27. This is 6.4 miles east of Topanga Canyon Blvd. and 3.8 miles west of the San Diego Freeway overpass.

Walk around the fireroad gate, then west along a one-half mile long ridge. There are steep firebreaks to the west and to the south. The west firebreak leads down to Mulholland Drive in a very steep 400' drop. The south firebreak follows a ridge separating two forks of the stream in upper Rustic Canyon. The Bent Arrow Trail has its beginning below the south crest of the ridge about 300 yards from the west end. The Bee Tree Trail has its eastern terminals farther out on the firebreak and makes a steep descent west to Rustic Canyon.

The views from Peaks 1927 and 1960 are worthwhile. Some exceptional sunsets can be seen from here. The San Fernando Valley stretches out to the north and on a clear day or night is spectacular. Caballero Canyon is below, and on the other side of the ridge to the northeast is Encino Reservoir, a part of the municipal water system. The immediate view south is of Rustic Canyon. Beyond is the ocean, the beach cities, Palos Verdes, and Santa Catalina Island. The view west shows some of Mulholland Drive and part of the Bent Arrow Trail.

This short side trip can be conveniently taken when driving Mulholland Drive between Sepulveda Blvd. and Topanga Canyon Blvd.

Not a part of this hike, but if you've driven here and all you get is a 30-minute stroll, you may want to try another. Go north, downhill on Fireroad 27 for 3/8 to 1/2 mile and look for an indistinct trail on the left going down Caballero East Fork. Follow this down to the subdivision and back. You might get another half hour walk. Of significant interest to botanists, the only known colony of Rabbit-brush (*Chrysothamnus nauseosus*) in the Santa Monica

Mountains is in this canyon. Or was — I should say. A subdivision has eliminated the lower part of the trail and brush clearing is likely to wipe out this uncommon plant.

You also might want to hike down Fireroad 27 to get a good look at Encino Reservoir. The north end of Fireroad 27 ends in a residential area. Coming back uphill on 27 is a good workout.

GIZMO PEAK

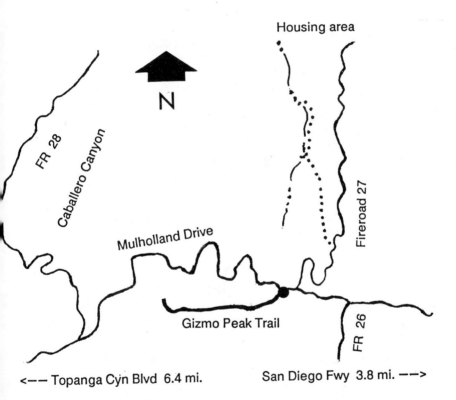

SKULL ROCK LOOP

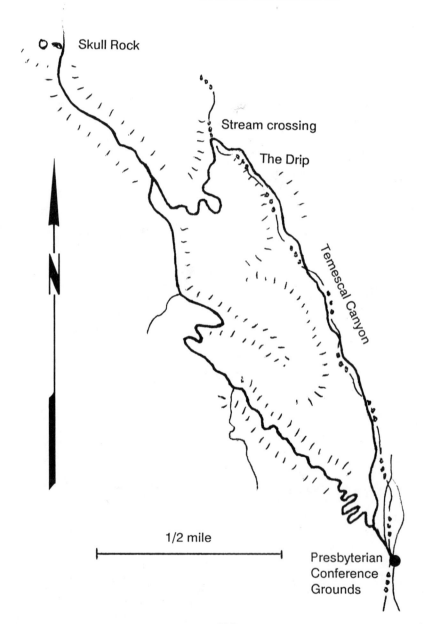

Skull Rock

Stream crossing

The Drip

Temescal Canyon

1/2 mile

Presbyterian
Conference
Grounds

N

HIKE 19

Distance:	4.5 miles
Elevation:	1050' gain and loss
Terrain:	Rocky, steep trail and a rock scramble stream crossing
Time:	2 hours
Trailhead:	Temescal Canyon (#16)

The trail upstream from Temescal Canyon trailhead once was a fireroad, but you might question the statement as you approach the waterfall. Rocks and erosion have remade the road into a mountain trail.

Future plans call for a parking area on the north side of Sunset Boulevard. For the present, drive north on Temescal Canyon Road and park at the Presbyterian Conference Center. For the privilege of hiking across private property we sign in and out. Read and abide by the posted rules. An information booth has an attendant on weekends.

Walk upstream on the trail past a house with a neat vegetable garden and some chickens. The trail immediately turns left as it goes uphill. In about 100 feet a fork in the trail gives an option of a "View Point" or a "Waterfall." Today's hike is a loop and you will see everything enroute so either way will do. I turn right and go counterclockwise because the return trip allows a continuous changing panoramic view of the ocean and the city. After turning right the trail levels off to a degree and contours north along the side of a steep slope. Conference Center houses are below on the canyon floor. You will cross a dry side stream on a wooden bridge, and soon angle down to the flat ground in the canyon.

You will notice two steel girder dams. They were constructed in 1979 to control floods that have been a feature of this canyon for thousands of years. The plant community along this part of the hike is riparian woodland. Look for willows, a few sycamores, and mule fat. A stand of french broom (*Cytisus monspessulanus)* grows on a slightly elevated bank near the trail. We see other introduced plants, giving us a clue to the upper limit of habitation in this otherwise wild canyon. The cliff-forming pebble-cobble conglomerate rock seen on both walls was formed in a shallow, tropical sea during Paleocene and Eocene epochs (40 - 70 million years ago). This massive rock formation dominates the canyon, and its hardness accounts for the spectacular steep cliffs.

About 30 minutes into the hike the trail begins a climb above the stream on the right slope. This pulls you out of the shade of the riparian woodland and into a chaparral plant community. Once out of the canyon the rest of the hike is in chaparral. About 35 minutes into the hike you pass a waterfall named "The Drip." Usually it isn't even wet, but after a good rain you will get drenched because the trail is close. Notice the calcium carbonate (limestone) layer on the face of the falls. This deposit is the result of evaporation over a great period of time. Rainwater becomes slightly acidic when it soaks through decomposing leaves, and picks up some carbon. If this dilute carbonic acid filters through sandstone it can leach out some of the calcium. Evaporation causes a film to build on the rock surface.

Five minutes after passing The Drip you will come to the final crossing of Temescal Creek. A wooden bridge, once suitable for vehicular traffic, crossed at this point. On 23 October 1978 a fire swept Temescal Canyon and burned the bridge and all the vegetation on both ridges about the canyon (see fire history map on pages 128-129). The fire spared streamside vegetation. Climbing the rocks on the other side is the toughest part of this hike.

If you are warmed-up at this point you can get a good ten minute workout before cutting left on an intersecting trail that heads south along the crest of a ridge. However, in order that this be a Skull Rock loop you would not turn onto the side trail but continue north for 8 to 10 minutes to Skull Rock. Climb around the rock and photograph it then return to the trail that goes along the ridge.

California buckwheat and California sagebrush dominate the ridge with some laurel sumac and black sage spotted throughout. As you walk south, big-pod ceanothus makes an appearance, and upon starting down the south facing slope the 8' high ceanothus takes over completely. The trail starts downhill after you have walked along the ridge for ten minutes. Views of the ocean are great. Palos Verdes Peninsula and Santa Catalina Island are usually visible. Sometimes the skyscrapers of Los Angeles aren't hidden in smog, making an interesting contrast of scenery. Part way down the ridge the trail makes a 90° right turn and contours west to another ridge. Upon reaching the ridge, the trail makes a 90° left turn to continue back to Temescal Canyon trailhead. In several places side trails lead west and are used by locals. These side trails are usually steep, some are overgrown. Stay on the main trail.

James P. Kenney

Skull Rock is a good place to rest or to look around. Kids like to climb through the "eye," and so do some of us who are kids at heart.

EAGLE SPRING, TEMESCAL FIREROAD
SANTA YNEZ CANYON LOOP

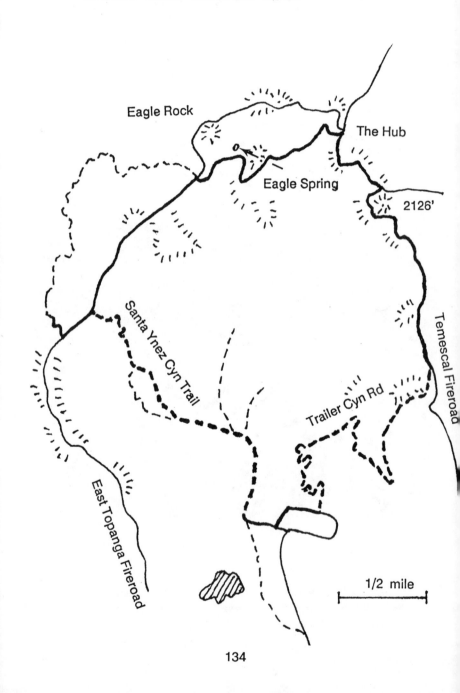

Eagle Rock

The Hub

Eagle Spring

2126'

Santa Ynez Cyn Trail

Temescal Fireroad

Trailer Cyn Rd

East Topanga Fireroad

1/2 mile

HIKE 20

Distance:	10 miles roundtrip
Elevation:	1800' gain and loss
Terrain:	Fireroad and trail
Time:	4 hours 20 minutes
Trailhead:	Trippet Ranch (#1)

On Highway 27 just north of the town of Topanga turn east on Entrada Road. Once on Entrada Road, turn left at every street intersection. It is 1.1 miles to the entrance of Topanga State Park. Park your car.

From the east end of the parking lot follow a trail up the hill on the right. Go a quarter mile to an intersection called the "Latitude" to a sign labelled "Backbone Trail." Turn left onto the Eagle Spring Road, go 1½ miles to another road junction (Eagle Junction), take either road. The road to the left gains some elevation right away and gets up on a ridge overlooking Garapito Canyon on the north and Santa Ynez Canyon on the south. The road to the right drops down to Eagle Spring. Either the upper road or the lower road is the same distance between Eagle Junction and "The Hub"—1.4 miles. Four roads join at The Hub — Fireroad 30 coming south from Mulholland Drive, north loop Eagle Road, south loop Eagle Road, and Temescal Fireroad. If this loop trip is to take 4 hours and 20 minutes you should reach The Hub in 1 hour and are due for a ten minute rest. An interesting resting spot is in the "Cathedral Rock" area two minutes south on Temescal Fireroad.

Cathedral Rock may be reached by going past it on the road, then by cutting to the left and back. Go up a steep slope to a gap in the rocks. The atmosphere within Cathedral Rock is one of feeling snug, serenely comfortable, secure. You can quickly change this aura by going to the edge of the cliff and looking onto Rustic Canyon. The view of Rustic is an unusual display of steep chaparral covered slopes in a near primitive state. We will see this wild and beautiful country closer on other hikes.

The junction with Rogers Road is 10 minutes south on Temescal Fireroad. One hundred yards farther is a firebreak on the left that goes up to Peak 2126, the highest point in Topanga State Park. As you continue, a short spur road on the right goes to Peak 2036. A sign nearby states "T.S.P. 4 miles." Continue south on Temescal Fireroad another half mile. Almost immediately a road junction appears. The fork on the right is Trailer Canyon Road, and is the way down into Santa Ynez Canyon.

Trailer Canyon Road winds around a lot on the way down to Santa Ynez Canyon and drops 1300'. The road bottoms out in a housing area.

Overlooking Rustic Canyon from Cathedral Rock

Turn right on Michael Lane, following it several hundred yards until reaching a cross street, Vereda De La Montura. Turn right and follow it to the streambed.

A well-used trail goes upstream, gently for awhile, about a mile. There are several caves in the sandstone cliffs on both sides of the stream. A trail forks to the right going up quarry canyon. Stay to the left at this fork and the next one also. The trail follows the west fork of the stream through a dense riparian woodland until it takes an abrupt right turn and goes uphill steeply. Within 100 feet the trail is out of the canyon environment and in chaparral. The trail is steep uphill for an 800' gain in about a mile.

Upon reaching the Eagle Spring Road, turn left and return to the parking lot.

WHERE TO SEE
GEOLOGICAL FORMATIONS IN THE PARK

The oldest rock formation exposed in Topanga State Park is Santa Monica slate, a dark-gray and bluish-gray-to-black slate. This bedrock of the Santa Monicas was laid down during the Jurassic Period between 140 and 180 million years ago. Extensive exposures of the slate are visible in the central part of the mountains and extend into the eastern border of the Park. Good examples are found along Mulholland Drive, Sullivan Canyon and Rustic Canyon. One location of particular interest is reached by parking at Trailhead #10 and walking a few hundred feet west on

Mulholland to the roadcut. Here Santa Monica slate is overlaid by Modelo shale, 10-12 million years ago, (Miocene). The 130 million year gap in the geological history is explained mostly by erosion that occurred during periods of mountain uplift. An exposed fault zone in the same area

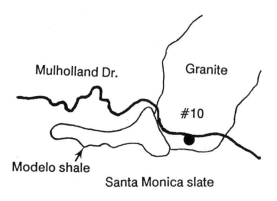

shows traces of orange colored "fault gouge" as evidence of the grinding power of the fault movement.

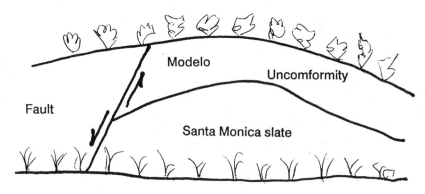

The parking area at Trailhead #10 sits on granite that intruded into the Santa Monica slate about 120 million years ago. The granite outcropping continues northeast toward Encino Reservoir and some granite is found as water-worn boulders in Rustic Canyon.

Tuna Canyon Formation is an Upper Cretaceous marine sequence of sandstone, siltstone and conglomerate deposited 70-120 million years ago. An example is found at Trailhead #6 and upstream .2 mile where it interfaces with Coal Canyon Formation at the Tuna Canyon thrust fault zone.

The 60-65 million-year-old (Paleocene) Coal Canyon Formation is a thick-bedded cobble conglomerate. Examples can be found in Topanga Creek (see Trailhead #6), along lower Santa Ynez Canyon Trail, in upper Los Liones Canyon and in the tributary beds of Garapito Creek. Reaching the Garapito tributaries can be something of a problem because there is no trail.

During the Oligocene Epoch (25-40 million years ago) the thick-bedded, massive sandstone and pebbly sandstone Sespe Formation was laid down when the Santa Monicas were above sea level. This nonmarine redbed sequence is distinctive because it is cliff-forming, often high on a ridge. Good examples are found in Topanga Canyon one mile north of Trailhead #6 and as a cliff on the east side of East Topanga Fireroad a little more than two miles south of Trippet Ranch. Much of the rock in Santa Ynez Canyon is Sespe.

Most of the rock exposed in the Park is Topanga Group. It is a thick sequence of sedimentary and volcanic rocks formed during the Miocene Epoch (12-20 million years ago). The sequence is divided into three units: Topanga Canyon Formation, Conejo Volcanics, and the Calabasas Formation. The Topanga Canyon Formation is sandstone sequence that overlies the Vaqueros Formation and underlies the Conejo Volcanics. It is further subdivided into 4 members.

The Conejo Volcanics is a thick sequence of volcanic rocks that began intruding into the existing sandstone about 15 million years ago and continued for about 2 million years.

The Calabasas Formation overlies the volcanics, and was probably laid down as a near continuous marine sedimentation. The Calabasas Formation is further subdivided into 6 members.

Eagle Rock is an outstanding example of Topanga Canyon Formation, but of equal interest is the volcanic intrusion to the southwest that is readily seen in the roadcut. The brown-colored diabase shows the typical concentric exfoliation in the "onion rock."

Station #16 on the Nature Trail at Trippet Ranch is at the base of a hill of basalt — also of volcanic origin but finer grained than diabase.

After leaving Trippet Ranch and turning right onto East Topanga Fireroad you will climb a hill of Calabasas Formation (sandstone). After going over the crest, look for "onion rock" diabase on the left. The next 1½ miles will be on either Topanga Canyon Formation (sandstone) or volcanic diabase.

Other examples of the Geologic Formations are in evidence throughout the Park. For a comprehensive explanation of the Geology, read bulletin 1457-E and the references cited there.

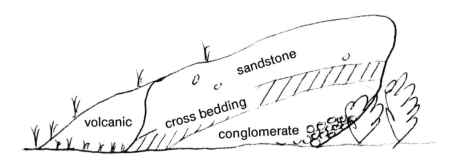

A rock formation along East Topanga Fireroad

Appendix A

LIST OF MAMMALS OF TOPANGA STATE PARK
common, technical and Indian names

Bobcat (*Lynx rufus*) To-koo' ut

Brush Rabbit (*Sylvilagus bachmani cinerescens*)

California Ground Squirrel (*Citellus beecheyi*) Hung-ē't

California Pocket Mouse (*Perognathus californicus*)

Coyote (*Canis latrans*) E'-tar'

Deer Mouse (*Peromyscus maniculatus*)

Desert Cottontail (*Sylvilagus audoboni*) Tŏ-so'-hut

Dusky-footed Woodrat (*Neotoma fuscipes*) Har"

Eastern Fox Squirrel (*Sciurus niger rufiventer*)

Gray Fox (*Urocyon cinereoargenteus californicus*)

Mountain Lion (*Felis concolor*) Too-koo'-rŏ't
(none seen recently)

Mule Deer (*Odocoileus hemionus californicus*) Soo-kaht"

Pacific Kangaroo Rat (*Dipodomys agilis*) 'Har"

Pocket Gopher (*Thomomys bottae*) Mhwat

Raccoon (*Procyon lotor*)

Striped Skunk (*Mephitus mephitus holzneri*) Po-ne'-vo

- (')   accented syllable
- (ˡ)   long sound to vowel or silent letter
- (ˢ)   at either end of syllable calls for an
      exploded sound
- (")   prolonged or trilled consonant

From Santa Monica Mountains Naturalists' Notebook by Sue Othmer.
List prepared by Barbara Smith.

Gabrieleno names from Indian Names for Plants and Animals by C.
Hart Merriam.

GEOLOGIC TIME SCALE AND SIGNIFICANT EVENTS

TOPANGA STATE PARK

Eras	Periods Epochs	time mya	Stratographic Nomenclature
C E N Z O I C	Quarternary Holocene	.01	alluvium landslides mudflows
	Pleistocene	3	
	Tertiary Pliocene	11	Modelo Formation
	Miocene		Topanga Group
		25	Vaqueros Formation
	Oligocene	40	Sespe Formation
	Eocene	60	
	Paleocene	70	Coal Canyon Formation
M E S O Z O I C	Cretaceous	135	Tuna Canyon Formation Granite intrusions
	Jurassic	180	Santa Monica Slate

Appendix B

Character of rock formation	Where found in Topanga State Park
Silt, sand, & gravel in streambeds bedrock & surficial materials fine grained mud and clay	Meadow N. of Trippet Ranch
Platy diatomaceous shale, mudstone, siltstone, sandstone	Gizmo Peak, Extreme NW corner of park along Mulholland Drive
Sedimentary & volcanic rocks in a thick heterogeneous sequence. Sediments are mostly sandstone; igneous are mostly basalt & diabase.	Eagle Rock (sedementary) Eagle Rock Rd (volcanic) intrusion seen in roadcut East Topanga Fireroad
Marine sandstone interbedded with siltstone & mudstone	
Non-marine thick-bedded massive sandstone	East Topanga Fireroad Santa Ynez Canyon
Thick-bedded cobble conglomerate	Topanga Creek Santa Ynez Canyon
Thick-bedded sandstone, containing slate or siltstone, siltstone and local conglomerate	Topanga Cr.(trailhead #6)
Granite and granidiorite	Mulholland Dr(trailhead #10)
Dark-gray to black slate	Mulholland Drive Sullivan Cyn, Rustic Cyn

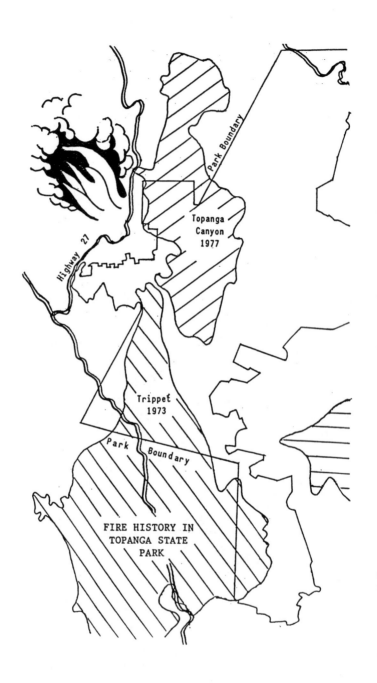

FIRE HISTORY IN
TOPANGA STATE
PARK

Topanga
Canyon
1977

Trippet
1973

Highway 27

Park Boundary

Park Boundary

Mulholland Drive

Park

Appendix C

Mandeville
1978

Park Boundary

Sunset Blvd

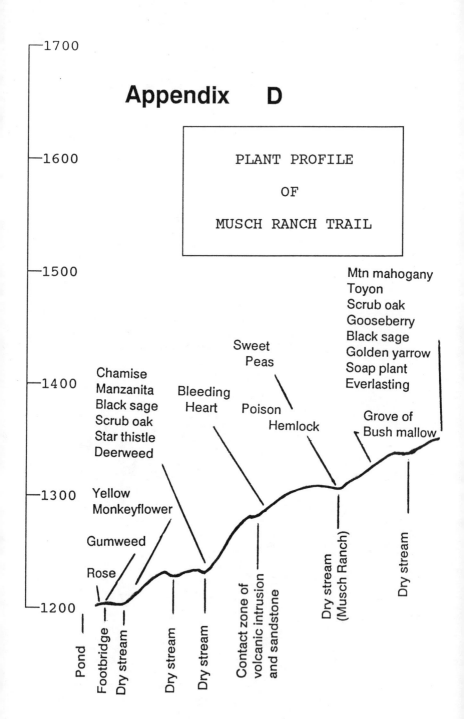

Appendix   D

PLANT PROFILE

OF

MUSCH RANCH TRAIL

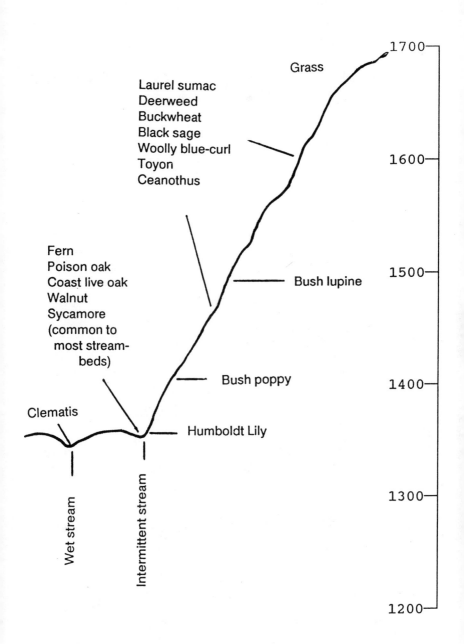

Grass

Laurel sumac
Deerweed
Buckwheat
Black sage
Woolly blue-curl
Toyon
Ceanothus

Fern
Poison oak
Coast live oak
Walnut
Sycamore
(common to
most stream-
beds)

Clematis

Bush lupine

Bush poppy

Humboldt Lily

Wet stream

Intermittent stream

1700

1600

1500

1400

1300

1200

RARE PLANTS OF THE SANTA MONICA MOUNTAINS FOUND IN SANTA YNEZ CANYON

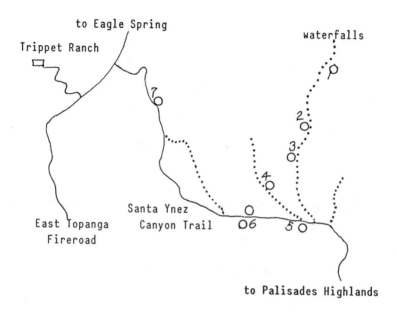

1. Stream orchid *(Epipactis gigantea)*

2. Coast boykinia *(Boykinia elata)*

3. Evening primrose *(Denothera hookeri)*

4. Summer holly *(Comarostaphylis diversifolia)*

5. Cream bush *(Holodiscus discolor)* Ocean spray

6. Canyon lupine *(Lupinus latifolius)*

7. Toadflax *(Linaria canadensis)*

Information on rare plants furnished by Jim Kenney.

PARTIAL LIST OF PLANTS FOUND IN SANTA YNEZ CANYON
(This is typical of other areas in the Park.)

STREAMSIDE AND DEEP SHADE

Flowers

*Coast boykinia (*Boykinia elata*)	March-April
Common monkeyflower (*Mimulus guttatus*)	March-May
Humboldt lily (*Lilium humboldtii*)	June-July
Leather root (*Psoralea macrostachya*)	June-Oct.
Maidenhair fern (*Adiantum jordanii*)	
Scarlet monkeyflower (*Mimulus cardinalis*)	June-Aug.
*Stream orchid (*Epipactis giganteum*)	May-June
Willow-herb (*Epilobium adenocaulon*)	June-Oct.
Woodland star (*Lithophragma affine*)	April-May

Shrubs
Mule-fat (*Baccharis viminea*)
Willow (*salix spp.*)

CANYON

Flowers

Blue larkspur (*Delphinium patens*)	March-April
Bush monkeyflower (*Diplacus longiflorus*)	April-June
California fuchsia (*Zauschneria cana*)	Aug.-Oct.
*Canyon lupine (*Lupinus latifolius*)	May-June
Canyon sunflower (*Venegasia carpesoides*)	March-July
Caterpillar phacelia (*Phacelia cicutaria*)	March-June
Clarkia (*Clarkia unguiculata*)	May-June
Climbing penstemon (*Penstemon cordifolius*)	*June-July*
Crimson sage (*Salvia spathacea*)	April-June
*Evening primrose (*Denothera hookeri*)	June-Aug.
Farewell to spring (*Clarkia deflexa*)	May-June
Globe lily (*Calochortus albus*)	April-May
Goldenrod (*Solidago calif.*)	July-Oct.
Hedge nettle (*Stachys bullata*)	March-May
Indian paintbrush (*Castilleja foliosa*)	March-June
Indian pink (*Silene laciniata*)	May-June
Live forever (*Dudleya lanceolata*)	April-June
Live forever (*Dudleya pulverulenta*)	Aug.-Sept.

Morning glory (*Calystegia macrostegia*)	All year
Owl's clover (*Orthocarpus purpurascens*)	April-May
Phacelia (*Phacelia grandiflora*)	May-June
Sticky phacelia (*Phacelia viscida*)	March-June
Wild onion (*Allium haematochiton*)	April-May

Shrubs

Chaparral currant (*Ribes malvaceum*)	Dec.-Feb.
Coffeeberry (*Rhamnus californica*)	May-June
Elderberry (*Sambucus mexicana*)	April-July
Fuchsia-flowering gooseberry (*Ribes speciosum*)	Jan.-March
Honeysuckle (*Lonicera subspicata*)	April-June
Mugwort (*Artemesia douglasii*)	July-Nov.
*Ocean-spray (*Holodiscus discolor*)	May-July
Poison-oak (*Toxicodendron diversilobum*)	March
Snowberry (*Symphoricarpos mollis*)	April-May
Spanish broom (*non-native*)(*Spartium junceum*)	April-June
*Summer holly (*Comarostaphylis diversifolia*)	April
Wild rose (*Rosa californica*)	April-June

Trees

California bay (*Umbellularia californica*)
California walnut (*Juglans californica*)
Coast live oak (*Quercus agrifolia*)
Sycamore (*Platanus racemosa*)

* Rare plants of the Santa Monica Mountains but found in
   Santa Ynez Canyon

RIDGES AND HIGHER SLOPES

Wildflowers

Blue dicks (*Dichelostemma pulchella*)	March-May
Blue-eyed grass (*Sisyrinchium bellum*)	March-May
California poppy (*Eschscholzia spp.* [2])	March-May
Canchalagua (*Centaurium venustum*)	May-June
Cliff aster (*Malocothrix saxatilis*)	March-Sept.
Everlasting (*Gnaphalium spp.*)	March-Oct.
Four o'clock (*Mirabilis laevis*)	March-May
Golden yarrow (*Eriophyllum confertiflorum*)	April-June

Lupine *(Lupinus spp.)*	March-May
Mariposa lily *(Calochortus catalinae)*	March-April
Mariposa lily *(Calochortus plummerae)*	June-July
Peony *(Paeonia californica)*	Jan.-March
Popcorn flower *(Cryptantha intermedia)*	March-May
Scarlet bugler *(Penstemon centranthifolius)*	April-May
Scarlet larkspur *(Delphinium cardinale)*	June-July
Showy penstemon *(Penstemon spectabilis)*	May-June
Soap plant *(Chlorogalum pomeridianum)*	June
Star lily *(Zygadenus fremontii)*	April-May
Sticky snapdragon *(Antirrhinum multiflorum)*	May-June
Western thistle *(Cirsium coulteri)*	April-May
Yellow monkeyflower *(Mimulus brevipes)*	April-May

Shrubs

Big Pod ceanothus *(Ceanothus megacarpus)*	Feb.-March
Black sage *(Salvia mellifera)*	April-June
Bush lupine *(Lupinus longifolius)*	April-June
Bush mallow *(Malacothamnus fasciculatus)*	June-Aug.
Bush poppy *(Dendromecon rigida)*	April-July
Bush sunflower *(Encelia californica)*	March-June
California buckwheat *(Eriogonum fasciculatum)*	May-July
Chamise *(Adenostoma fasciculatum)*	May-June
Coastal buckwheat *(Eriogonum cinereum)*	Aug.-Sept.
Deerweed *(Lotus scoparius)*	March-July
Goldenbush *(Haplopappus spp.)*	October
Holly-leaf cherry *(Prunus ilicifolia)*	April-May
Laurel sumac *(Rhus laurina)*	June-July
Mountain Mahogany *(Cercocarpus betuloides)*	April
Purple sage *(Salvia leucophylla)*	May-June
Redheart ceanothus *(Ceanothus spinosus)*	March-April
Sagebrush *(Artemesia californica)*	September
Scrub oak *(Quercus dumosa)*	
Sugar bush *(Rhus ovata)*	May-June
Toyon *(Heteromeles arbutifolia)*	May-July
Woolly blue-culs *(Trichostema lanatum)*	April-June
Yucca *(Yucca whipplei)*	May-June

TRIPPET RANCH AREA

These plants are not common in the rest of the Park but are common on Trippet Ranch.

Buttercup (*Ranunculus californica*)	March-April
Goldenbush, Palmers (*Haplopappus palmeri*)	October
Red maids (*Calendrinia menziesii*)	March-April
Turkey mullein (*Eremocarpus setigerus*)	June
Vinegar weed (*Trichostema lanceolatum*)	June-July

MUSCH RANCH TRAIL

Except for the rare plants found in Santa Ynez Canyon most of the same plants are also found along the Musch Ranch Trail. In addition, Bleeding heart (*Dicentra ochroleuca*) is found along the lower Musch Ranch Trail. The abundance or rarity of particular species is related to rainfall and most importantly, to the time and extent of previous fires.

The information in this appendix has been compiled by Jim Kenney. Jim states that he could "list hundreds more . . I've tried to limit to the most important ones."

Appendix E

PREHISTORIC MAN IN THE SANTA MONICA MOUNTAINS

YEARS AGO	PERIOD	CHARACTERISTICS
8500	Early Man	Hunters of large game animals Used spears with large stone point Were adaptive to a changing environment and toward the end of the period, emphasis became placed on use of grass, sage, and other small seeds. No evidence of burials in cemeteries
Coastal 3800	Milling-stone Horizon (Early Period)	Villages were established Hard small seeds processed by use of mano and metate A variety of food sources Less hunting of large animals by spear Vegetal sources increasingly important Late in the period, acorns became a source of food. Obsidian artifacts indicate some trade Shell beads and ornaments came into use Burials in the extended position
3000 Interior 1500	Inter-mediate Horizon	Cultural developments in a more structured society Coastal food resources grew in importance A shift from the emphasis on hard seed strategy to use of acorns took place, although hard seeds remained a staple into the Spanish period. Mortar and pestle became common Appearance of non-utilitarian artifacts Increased diversity of shell beads/ornaments Evidence of trading Canoe invented Burials were semi-flexed
	Late Horizon (Late Period)	Large villages Extended trade activity Bow and arrow introduced A money-based economy developed (500-800 AD) Burials were tightly flexed

Bibliography

BECK, W.A. and Y.D. Haase
    1974   Historical Atlas of California.
                Univ. of Okla. Press; Norman, Oklahoma

BLACKBURN, T.
    1963   Ethnohistoric description of Gabrieleno
                Culture.
                Archaeological Survey Annual report, UCLA

STATE OF CALIFORNIA DEPT OF PARKS AND RECREATION
    1977   Santa Monica Mountains State Parks,
                Topanga, Malibu Creek, and Point Mugu,
                Resource Management Plans, General Development
                Plans, and Environmental Impact Reports.

CLELAND, R.C.
    1951   The Cattle on a Thousand Hills.
                The Ward Richie Press, L.A., California

GREENE, Linda W.
    1980   Historical Overview of Santa Monica Mountains
                National Recreation Area.
                U.S. Dept. of the Interior, National Park
                Service. Historic Preservation Branch.

HEARST, Peter
    1979   Conceptual Trail System for the Santa Monica
                Mountains.
                S.M. Mtns State Parks Advis. Committees

HEIZER, R.F. and E.M. Lemert
    1947   Observations on Archaeological Sites in Topanga
                Canyon, California.
                U.C. Press

HEIZER, R.F.
    1978   Handbook of N. American Indians, Vol. 8
                Smithsonian Institution

HOOTS, H.W.
  1931   Geology of the Eastern Part of the Santa Monica
            Mountains, Los Angeles County, California.
            U.S. Government Printing Office

JOHNSON, Keith L.
  1962   Site LAn-2 A Late Manifestation of the Topanga
            Complex in S. California Prehistory.
            Thesis for Master of Arts in Anth., UCLA

LOS ANGELES TIMES
  Various dates from 2/7/71 — 8/14/74

LEVY, Lou
  undated   Day Walks in the Santa Monica Mountains.
            SMMTF of the L.A. Chapter, Sierra Club

McAULEY, Milt
  1987   Hiking Trails of the Santa Monica Mountains.
            Canyon Publishing Co., Canoga Park, California

MERRIAM, C. Hart
  1979   Indian Names for Plants and Animals.
            Among Californian and other Western North American
            Tribes.
            Ballena Press, Socorro, New Mexico

NICKLES, Francis
  1980   The Santa Ynez Canyon and Vicinity Trail Guide.
            Marina Printing, Marina Del Rey, California

OTHMER, Sue — editor
  1980   Santa Monica Mountains Naturalists' Notebook.

RAVEN, Peter H. and Henry J. Thompson
  1977   Flora of the Santa Monica Mountains, California.
            University of California, Los Angeles

ROBINSON, W.W.
  1962   Santa Monica.
            Title Insurance and Trust Co., Los Angeles

SIERRA CLUB
1974   Symposium on Living with the Chaparral.
            Sierra Club, San Francisco, California

SUDWORTH, George B.
1908   Forest Trees of the Pacific Slope.
            U.S. Government Printing Office

TREGANZA, A.E. and C.G. Malamud
1950   The Topanga Culture First Season's Excavation of
            the Tank Site, 1947 (LAn-1).
            Anthropological Records Vol. 20 #2
            U.C. Press

USDA, FOREST SERVICE
1977   Proceedings of the Symposium on the Environmental
            Consequences of Fire and Fuel Management in
            Mediterranean Ecosystems.

U.S. DEPT OF THE INTERIOR. GEOLOGICAL SURVEY
            Maps 7½ minute series (topographic).

U.S. DEPT OF THE INTERIOR. NATIONAL PARK SERVICE
            Santa Monica Mountains National Recreation
            Area/California
1980   Draft Environmental Impact Statement and General
            Management Plan.

UCLA DEPARTMENT OF ANTHROPOLOGY
            Archaeological Survey Annual Report (var).

YERKES, R.F. et al
1973   Preliminary Geologic Map of the Unincorporated part
            of the Topanga Quadrangle.
            L.A. County, California

YERKES, R.F. and R.H. Campbell
1979   Stratigraphic Nomenclature of the Central Santa
            Monica Mountains, L.A. County, California.
            Geological Survey Bulletin 1457-E.
            U.S. Government Printing Office

Books by Milt McAuley

Hiking Trails of the Santa Monica Mountains

Hiking in Topanga State Park

Hiking Trails of Point Mugu State Park

Hiking Trails of Malibu Creek State Park

Wildflowers of the Santa Monica Mountains

Wildflower Walks of the Santa Monica Mountains

Guide to the Backbone Trail

THE AUTHOR

MILT McAULEY is a hiker, an author and a photographer. His seven books have been well-received by the hiking community of the Santa Monica Mountains. He and his wife Maxine regularly lead seven-mile hikes in the Santa Monica Mountains. Outdoor interests include botany, archaeology and the selective preservation of open space.

HIKING IN TOPANGA STATE PARK by Milt McAuley, has been written with both the new, as well as the experienced, hiker in mind. Invaluable information on Park entrances, trails and history will open the doors to many hours of outdoor recreation in our local Park.

COVER PICTURES

Front: Eagle Rock
Back: Santa Ynez Canyon Trail
by Milt and Maxine McAuley